CELEBRATING THE CENTENARY

CELEBRATING THE CENTENARY

ROYAL LYMINGTON YACHT CLUB

UNICORN

Dedication

I am immensely grateful to numerous individuals for assistance in the production of this Centenary book. With apologies to anyone who I have unintentionally failed to mention, here is a brief list of notable helpers:

Titch Blachford, Tony Blatchford, Peter Bruce, Graham Clarke, Mike Derrick, Neil Eccles, Ruth Evans, Richard Field, Roger Hawkes, Michael Hobson, Geoff Holmes, Ali Husband, Jonathan Hutchinson, Ado Jardine, Rosemary Johnson, Brian May, Malcolm McKeag, Dick Moore, Martin Nash, Jose Nieves, Sally Potter-Kalis, Ken Robinson, Hattie Rogers, Nick Ryley, Gordon Stredwick, Michael Webb, Jenny Wilson, Pippa Wilson, Roger Wilson, all the Circumnavigators, Kirsty Husband and her team at the Club, and, of course, Ian Strathcarron of Unicorn Publishing. I am (we are) also indebted to the work done by past Club Historian / Archivist Anthony Ruffell to create, curate and strengthen our archive, which has proved such a wonderful source for this book.

In addition, thanks are due to the volunteers who managed our Centenary preparations, particularly past Vice Commodore Robin Taunt, current VC Stephen Crates, and the Centenary Management team: Pauline Crates, Emma McEwen, Jenny and Roger Wilson and Nick Ryley. Thank you.

John Tudor

The Royal Lymington Yacht Club is one of the most active 'Royal' Clubs founded in the hopeful days after the first World War. Since then, the Club has gone from strength to strength, promoting racing, cruising and social events, as more members joined. As Patron of The Royal Lymington Yacht Club, I am always impressed to see the three burgees epitomising the stages of the Club's progression from a small river sailing club, to what it is today, and which symbolise the vision and energy of the founder, Major Cyril Potter. Likewise, when I see the picture of your first and only lady Commodore, The Honourable Mrs. Cecil Brownlow, I am reminded that she was a formidable person who concluded her predecessor's work, in obtaining the Royal Warrant, and who maintained the spirit of the Club during the difficult years of the Second World War.

The Club's Honours Boards proudly highlight the exploits and achievements of your Olympians, circumnavigators, racing and cruising sailors, and of course the juniors. One of the most distinctive features of The Royal Lymington has been its dedication to training, sailing education, and the exemplary Wednesday Junior Sailing, with its outreach to the children across the whole community.

One of the most notable racing achievements, from the 1970s to the 1990s, was The Royal Lymington Cup. This match-racing event, pitting expert crews against each other from clubs from across the world, championed 'on the water' race observing and became the premier event of the sailing season. Ashore, the unique feature of the Clubhouse is the glittering Pottership Trophy given by the Club's founder and competed for in the annual race for all Members.

I send you my very best wishes for your Centenary in 2022.

Anne

Published in 2022 by Unicorn
an imprint of Unicorn Publishing Group LLP
Charleston Studio
Meadow Business Centre
Lewes BN8 5RW
www.unicornpublishing.org

Text © named authors
Cover art © Sue Stitt
Images © Sportography: pages: 2, 4, 12, 121, 131, 132, 133, 134,
139, 140, 141, 142, 143, 144/5, 146/7, 148/9, 152, 224, 225,
226, 227, 228/9, 230, 231. Coolhat: pages 38, 54, 55, 118/9,
126/7, 165, 166/7, 194, 198, 238/9. Wessex photo: Page 174.
Alamy: page 184. SailGP: page 222. Hattie Rogers Sailing: pages
219, 220, 221. RLymYC members: pages 52, 112, 113, 114/5, 116,
117, 120, 122, 153, 154/5, 158, 160, 162, 168/9, 170/1, 192,
195, 196, 202, 214, 216/7, 240.

All rights reserved. No part of the contents of this book may be
reproduced, stored in or introduced into a retrieval system, or
transmitted, in any form or by any means (electronic, mechanical,
photocopying, recording or otherwise), without the prior written
permission of the copyright holder and the above publisher of
this book.

Every effort has been made to trace copyright holders and to obtain
their permission for the use of copyrighted material. The publisher
apologises for any errors or omissions and would be grateful to be
notified of any corrections that should be incorporated in future
reprints or editions of this book.

ISBN 978-1-914414-89-3

10 9 8 7 6 5 4 3 2 1

Designed by Guy Callaby
Printed by Fine Tone Ltd

Contents

Celebrating the Centenary

Introduction by the current Commodore Phil Lawrence and past Vice Commodore John Tudor

Prince Phillip, Prince Charles, Uffa Fox and sailing master Alastair Easton, 1958

2022 is an incredibly special year for our Club as we celebrate 100 years since its foundation in 1922. Throughout our Centenary year we have planned a programme of celebrations, building on our existing successful annual events, on and off the water, including a Centenary Regatta Day with "Après Sail" Festival and a spectacular Centenary Party.

It was in 1922 that the Lymington River Sailing Club was formed in the aftermath of the Great War which had frustrated all previous attempts to bring together local sailors. Many of "the great and the good" lived in Lymington and were members of the Royal Yacht Squadron in Cowes but they wanted their own Club on their home river. That year, Major Cyril Potter and his friends got together at Potter's house, near the ferry terminal, to form the Club.

They bought the disused Coastguard Boathouse which was ideally situated on the town side of the river. Since then, it has been expanded to become the excellent facility enjoyed by members today. "Royal" status was bestowed on the Club in 1938 which complemented Royal patronage of the Club since 1925, the current Patron being HRH The Princess Royal.

The Club currently has about 2,300 members and offers facilities to enable a wide range of waterborne activities from yachting and motor boating to dinghy racing and paddle-boarding. Ashore, the Club offers a 7-day catering service and many activities for Club members: quiz nights, bridge, yoga, lectures, photography exhibitions, art competitions etc. and, of course, a number of lunches, dinners and parties. We declared that the Centenary would try to be "all things to all members". During our long history we have aspired to promote yachting and waterborne activities in all forms. This book explains what we have achieved in the last 100 years. We hope you enjoy it.

*Possibly the best
view in the Solent*

1 How the Club Became Royal

Graham Clark, Club Historian, reflects on the campaign to turn the Lymington River Sailing Club into the Royal Club we know today...

It is entirely appropriate in the Club's Centenary year, to reflect on how the reborn Lymington River Sailing Club of 1922 blossomed into the RLymYC of today. There were two powerful and important founder Members of the Club: Major Cyril Potter and the Hon. Mrs Cecil Brownlow – Angela – both of whose memorable sketches grace the western end of the Island/ Needles Room. Between them, they are responsible for the birth and development of the Club and, in Mrs Brownlow's case, its care during the war.

From its energetic early days at Blakes, Potter's house near the entrance to the car-ferry pier, huge strides were made to establish the Club, as both a shore-based entity and its increasingly important position as a source of waterborne activity. Potter was a man of vision, energy and ambition: from the outset, he wanted the Club to develop and be recognised as an eminent home of yachting in the western Solent. It was no surprise, therefore, that he should want that recognition to include the accolade of becoming a royal yacht club.

As a Royal Yacht Squadron member, Potter had many connections, including royalty, that would provide the entrée to fulfil his ambition, but it took time, persuasion and the ultimate engagement of the Club's first lady Commodore – in the form of Mrs Brownlow – to bring the plan to fruition. One has only to visualise the two protagonists to imagine the different styles

Opposite:
HRH Prince Henry,
Duke of Gloucester,
our first Patron in 1926

Above:
Major Cyril Potter,
OBE, Founder,
Commodore
1922–37

Below:
The Hon. Mrs Cecil
Brownlow,
Commodore
1937–46

they employed to achieve the honour: Major Potter, the tough visionary, and his successor, Angela Brownlow, the charming mediator.

Potter, with his military background, would undoubtedly have regarded it as a campaign to obtain royal status for the Club. The process of doing so – and the Club was the youngest to become a royal yacht club – is opaque, to say the least. It mostly involves departments of state within government, but with reference to the Palace along the way. As might be imagined, Potter had friends in high places and he used those connections to further the campaign. This started as far back as 1925, with the Club only three years old but already with 300 Members – and still known as the Lymington River Sailing Club. The opening salvo from Potter was to the Home Secretary, setting out his stall, seeking the royal title and a defaced red ensign (then, as now, an unusual combination). By the end of 1925, the Admiralty Warrant had been approved for the Club to wear the defaced ensign from 1926, when it became the Lymington Yacht Club. The red ensign was adorned solely with the ship of Lymington on the fly (the naval crown appeared later, when royal status was granted).

Many exchanges took place in the royal application process, looking, amongst other things, at the standing and nature of the Club – its newness was commented upon – and consideration of other clubs that had received royal recognition and how Lymington's case compared with those. Among the measures used to assess if a club deserved royal status was the cumulative tonnage of its members' yachts. These messages, to and fro, contained many personal thoughts and comments, revealing a picture of some pressure from the Lymington end and some resistance from the London end, initially including the then Yacht Racing Association (YRA). Nothing in such matters moves swiftly and a degree of lobbying behind the scenes might have been thought necessary but, equally, could be regarded as unhelpful. Indications were received that the King (George V – very much the yachtsman) would be favourable, if the right recommendations were provided from government sources.

As the troops were being marshalled in the campaign, the personage of Maj. Gen. The Rt. Hon. J. B. Seely MP appears in correspondence: he was, during all this time, the Lord Lieutenant of Hampshire and, at the early stages, Vice-Commodore of the Club. Other heavyweights weighed in; senior officers of other yacht clubs wrote in support of Lymington (there was a lot of cross-membership of local clubs). The years rolled by; correspondence continued fitfully but still no conclusion was reached. Such was Potter's drive and connections that, as early as 1926, HRH Prince Henry, the Duke of Gloucester, accepted the invitation to become the Club's first Patron.

But still the years went by and the campaign moved slowly through the 1930s; almost annual skirmishes broke out, with the request for the royal title being renewed and declined, from time to time. One has to admire Cyril Potter's tenacity and thick skin – many a lesser mortal would have given up, but not he. Home Secretaries came and went but still Potter managed to find personal connections to keep his dream alive. By now, the YRA was in support, as was the Admiralty, so the signs were beginning to look a little more positive. Entrenched positions are difficult to reverse, however, and need something new and different for the matter to be reconsidered.

There were changes on the regal stage during 1936, with the arrival and departure of King Edward VIII followed by the accession of King George VI. This new age provided an opportunity for a new approach: this time, step forward Angela Brownlow, who, having become Commodore in 1937, and no doubt with connections of her own, made a new application. Once again, LYC membership (now 500) and the tonnage of their yachts were tallied. During the summer of 1938, when one or two other things were going on in world affairs, a final push was made for the royal title, with support from no less than the Commodore of the RYS and his Vice-Commodore (also VC of our Club), together with the Club's local MP.

On 3 November 1938, approval of the royal title was granted and the news communicated to the Commodore: so began the Royal Lymington Yacht Club. A few days prior, a private communication was made from the Home Secretary to Major Potter (at an address in Ipswich) advising him that his 13 years of effort had at last been successful (even if it had taken someone else to get the ball across the line). The Club owes a great debt – not just for such matters as its title – to those two titans of the formative years: Major Cyril Potter and the Hon. Mrs Cecil Brownlow.

From LRSC to RLymYC (RLYC being superseded in the 1980s)

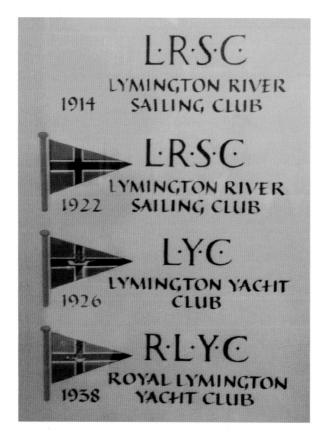

The evolution of the Club can be seen through the development of its burgee, to be found, framed, in the Clubhouse:

The Club was made aware of the details of this long process by the kind efforts of Mr David Prothero, whose close interest in matters concerning flags led him to research the Club in the National Archives at Kew. The report of his findings came out of the blue in 2008, for which the Club is enduringly grateful to him. Since then, a request to Kew was made, and generously funded, by Senior Trustee and former Commodore, Geoff Holmes, to obtain copies of every document concerning the Club held in the National Archive.

2 Inception – REV. V. K. C. Logan's History

By V. K. C. Logan, Winchester, 1968

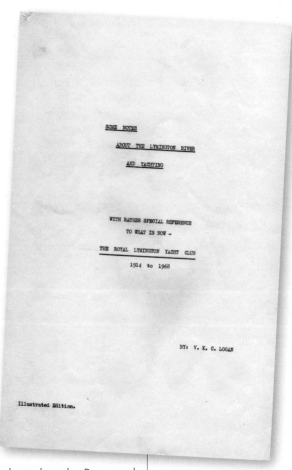

The Reverend Logan produced this short historical memoir as a 'souvenir of a very happy time', in September 1968. It was essentially based on his own memories, supported by data from the *Encyclopaedia Britannica* and conversations with his peers. These were of course pre-decimal times, and subscriptions were paid in guineas. It also fills some of the gaps missing from the Club's history caused by the loss of materials in the Great Flood of 1989.

He may well have been the local vicar in the 1920s, but when the Reverend Logan wrote his history in 1968, he was living in Winchester, so it must have been quite an expedition to re-visit Lymington in later life before the advent of the M3 and M27.

There is no doubt that there were yachts based in Lymington at the end of the 19th Century, but they presumably belonged to very wealthy people, and they were probably large craft used for cruising.

In 1912, when I was a boy, I was given a punt which I used on the river at Roydon where my father then lived. This punt had been made by a certain Major Stevens, who then lived at Passford Cottage; it was named *Mudlarklet* and I always understood that it had been used as a tender to Major Stevens' yacht, named *Mudlark*, and that it had been given to me because he had built a more suitable tender for himself. It had a tarred bottom and green topsides.

By 1914 I used to overhear talk of boats being called 'Prams' (later called Scows) to distinguish them from a later, larger craft which was given the name Pram.

1914 And The Lymington River Sailing Club

At the beginning of 1914, 14 people, of whom my father was one, founded a Lymington River Sailing Club. The original Members were joined by four more shortly after the start, making a total of 18. A hand booklet was produced, giving a list of Members and rules. In charge was Captain H. H. Nicholson (later of Creek Cottage); there was no Commodore. Captain Nicholson, who was a great seaman, was regarded with huge respect, and in the years after the First World War, with great affection, especially by the younger Members, for whom he did so much to help them with sailing.

This club was really a racing club for Prams, although in between the weekly races (held between May 15th and August 15th), Members cruised about the river and the Solent, and when the weather was suitable, going as far afield as Yarmouth and Newtown on the Isle of Wight.

There were also some Pram owners who were not Members of the Club. Prams were built either by Dan Bran or by the Berthon Boat Company, and, if I remember correctly, cost under £20 complete.

The First World War started on 4 August 1914 and closed down the Club before it could hold its final race of the season, or its first Annual General Meeting, due to be held in the autumn of that year.

The Club subscription was to be 10/- per annum (50p in today's money) payable on Lady Day; from this fund, prizes were awarded at the end of the season.

At this time, although I did not go afloat myself with my father, I was taken two or three times a week in summer to the Lymington Baths, and I do vaguely remember a few yachts larger than Prams being pointed out to me.

Yachting was still very much a private venture of the few, and I observe that Guide Books, even as late as 1924, do not mention any form of boating, although they do mention the baths and swimming.

To the general public at large, Lymington was only a 'jumping-off point' for the Isle of Wight.

1921 And The Lymington River Sailing Club

As soon as my father and others returned form the war, they acquired boats, and although we no longer lived near Lymington, we spent many summers in, or near.

My father acquired an ex Lee-on-the-Solent one design (*Ed. 16ft designed by Charles Nicholson*), which we named Water Wagtail; the 1914 Pram was also resurrected, and her name changed from *Loganberry* to *Water Rat*. We rather liked a little uniformity and followed the line taken by a family (I believe called Young), all of whose boats were named Kitti-something. In particular, I remember *Kittiwake* and *Kittihawk*. The punt *Mudlarklet* was also resurrected as tender to *Water Rat* and *Water Wagtail*, both of which were moored off Dan Bran's slipway. The Harbour dues were 5/- (25p today) per boat per year, and were collected by the harbour master (a Captain Harper), who pursued one in a duck punt for this purpose.

As there was no club we invented a burgee: a green pennant with a white border and a white ball in the centre. Later, when there was a club, this design, albeit in a square shape, became the Logan racing flag and personal flag, and was registered as a design with Lloyd's.

Those sailing on the river did not know each other and could at first only look at each other with curiosity; soon we were waving and shouting greetings, and eventually some names and addresses were exchanged. As a result, in the autumn of 1921, Major Cyril Potter OBE took a lead and invited all who might be interested to his house. He lived at Blakes, a house now known as Ferry Point. He had a number of boats and was a member of the Royal Yacht Squadron. At this meeting, which I attended, he proposed the formation of a Lymington River Sailing Club. The proposal was unanimously agreed to and in spring 1922, a Lymington River Sailing Club (second edition) came into being.

There was weekly racing for Prams and also for a handicap class; starting was from Major Potter's motor cruiser *Wendy*, his skipper (another Captain Harper) firing a shot gun into the air.

During 1922 a new class of boat arrived on the river, and by 1923 there were 17 of them, with more in Yarmouth. These formed themselves into a club and were called the Solent Sea Birds. They were delightful, especially for the young, as they were almost uncapsizable, even if the main sheets were made fast. They were built at Cowes, and cost £80 each complete. They were half decked,18 feet in length over all and sloop rigged.

My father purchased one named *Water Witch*. I was able to race in every race for the class when in the neighbourhood, and, with the aid of a few necessities, to camp aboard her and cruise locally. When I was not in the neighbourhood, a friend looked after her and raced her.

The highlight of that season was probably the Lymington Town Regatta held on 16 August 1922, which not only included races for LRSC boats but also for a great number and variety of visiting boats, together with many other events both interesting and amusing. Both *Water Rat* and *Water Witch* raced, and one of them won a prize.

On 3 April 1923, an Annual General Meeting was held at Major Potter's house, where it was learned that the then coastguard boathouse (there had been an earlier coastguard boathouse at Dan Bran's shed and slipway) was available for renting. It was unanimously decided to rent it and fit it out as a clubhouse. To do this, folding tables and chairs were purchased and partitions erected at the back of the building. I do remember two doors, one labelled 'galley', the other 'Ladies'. The first Steward and Boatman was a Mr Scamlon, an ex-stoker in the Royal Navy. Refreshments were very simple – tea made on a primus stove, biscuits and, I think, beer and minerals. The subscription went up to £2. 2. 0d for new Members (it had been £1 1.0d); half price for non-boat-owners and suitable reductions for non-port Members and junior Members etc.

Great events at this time included a Solent Classes Racing Association Regatta as well as a Town Regatta, the latter including a race for the J Class boats.

In 1923 through the kindness of the Commodore (Major Potter) I was able to invite the Cambridge University Cruising Club to hold their Marine Meeting at Lymington from August 27th to 31st. Their Commodore was H. Yale Oldham (a tutor at King's College). The event was notorious because of an almost total disregard of local advice on the first day; collisions with the ferry were frequent, and various minor disasters occurred, much to the horror of young LRSC Members who had lent their boats for the occasion. However, by the end of the event, harmony was restored, and a dinner was held at the Angel Hotel.

On Saturday 28 August 1923 the Club held its first regatta. This was highly successful and included races for many classes, including the 18ft International Class.

During the next ten years (1928 to 1938), a number of things happened which I cannot date with any precision, because I was only in Lymington for a few weeks every year; I therefore record them in the order that they come into my mind.

The Club adopted a burgee, the design of which has remained unchanged in spite of the fact that at its inception, there were many complaints about its similarity to the Norwegian flag: a red pennant with a blue cross and white cross and the Lymington ship in the centre of the cross. Later, a Neptune crown was added in the hoist. Some of the original Members formed the Club into a company, and then took out £100 shares which they gave back to the Club, allowing the premises to be bought rather than rented. (The names of these Members, done in illuminated gold leaf and suitably framed, were duly recorded for posterity. Some time after the Second World War I found that this item had been thrown out. At the time, I did not worry: I now think it was a pity.)

Many people replaced their sea birds with other craft, mostly West Solent Restricted Class. I replaced *Water Witch* with *Scoter*, a small cabin cruiser

27 feet LOA with a small cabin. The few remaining sea birds now raced in the handicap class.

The Club adopted a cap badge: a round shield, defaced at the top with a fouled anchor; within it the Lymington ship and, below, the letters LRSC. There was a large edition for men, a smaller one for ladies, and one set in a miniature merchant navy 'wreath' for professional skippers. At the time some Members made great objection to the shield being defaced by the fouled anchor, saying that this was heraldically incorrect.

A Club mess uniform was designed, and a coloured drawing of it exhibited. It consisted of a double-breasted navy-blue dinner jacket with royal blue facings, on which the skipper's badge was mounted. Black club buttons with a Lymington ship in a round shield were also produced, and have remained unchanged to this day except for changes in the letters underneath. I do not think that the mess jacket was ever ordered by anyone, although the younger Members greatly coveted it. I personally never saw one either at the first Club dinner or the first Club dance.

Members subscribed money to add a floor to the Club (the roof is original, having been jacked up course by course). (*Ed. It appears the roof was jacked up, a course at a time, as the first floor brick courses were laid. Jacking up full height at one go, would have been a bit risky!*)

Upstairs was a lounge-cum-ballroom with an alcove stage for a band; downstairs was a bar, ladies' room, gents' room with bath, a forecourt and a small galley, all done with wood partitions. The old sloping boat-launching slipway was replaced by a pier. This was a great asset as the slipway had to be scrubbed down after every high tide. A suitable flag staff with signal yard was also provided, and signal cannons were also bought.

A new Steward was appointed – a Mr Francis (a former Royal Marine). His wife acted as Stewardess, and simple meals could be obtained if ordered in advance. Mr and Mrs Francis constantly obliged everyone and were greatly liked. In those days there were bells labelled 'Steward' every few yards, and whenever they were rung, Mr Francis appeared at the double. He also acted as boatman and gunner. All who knew him were very sorry to hear of his death due to illness during the Second World War, and deeply sympathised with Mrs Francis.

The Club changed its name to the Lymington Yacht Club, and the subscription went up to £3 3. 0d with an entrance fee of £3 3. 0d for all new Members.

The Club was now firmly established, with regular racing, much cruising and its own annual regatta.

A further extension was added in the form of a north wing on land purchased from the Corporation; there was a forecourt in front, and at the back on what is now the Corporation Car Park was a Club dinghy park. The interior was entirely re-arranged to provide better and bigger accommodation. A starting platform was built on the Solent to avoid having to use a large yacht for regattas.

In 1926 His Royal Highness the Duke of Gloucester became Patron of the Club, the name changing to the Royal Lymington Yacht Club. Permission was obtained for a Club red ensign, with the Lymington ship surmounted by a Neptune crown in the fly.

At this point my memories cease, because I was out of England, overseas from 1938–45, and, except for one visit in 1946, I did not return to the Club until 1955.

The Second World War closed the Club and the premises were taken over by the Fire Service, but I have heard that a small group of senior

Certificate of Incorporation – Lymington River Sailing Club 1924

4 Scows sailing in the Lymington River off the Town Quay

Members kept things going by lunching once a week at the Mayflower Hotel.

However, one day in the summer of 1946 I did visit Lymington, and I was walking around the empty building when I met Captain Mostyn Williams, who told me that the Club had been de-requisitioned, and he and some other Members were trying to get things going again. To cut a long story short, with much hard work, they succeeded. (Much of the hard work was, I believe, done by the Members themselves, in view of the rationing of paint, materials and labour at this time.)

Racing and cruising began again, and surpassed former standards. Various social events were started and grew successfully; lunching at the Club became a regular thing for those who lived locally. The work done by Mr and Mrs Francis was now undertaken by a staff of barman, cook, boatman etc. The bells were disconnected and finally removed.

Now, in 1968, the building is being further modernised and enlarged, and because no fresh land is available, the enlargement is over the original forecourt. Although the work is incomplete at the time of writing these notes, one can see the result is going to be very good.

During the years the Club badge has been changed – no longer 'a fouled anchor fouls it'. It is simply an oval shield containing Neptune's crown at the top, with below it a Lymington ship and the letters RLYC.

The mess jacket is no longer heard of but there are suitable badges for putting onto the lapels of an ordinary dinner jacket. The present subscription is £5 5. 0d with a £10 10. 0d entrance fee for new Members, with reductions for junior and family Members.

By V. K. C. Logan
Winchester 1968

3 Early Club Yachting in Lymington

Club Historian Graham Clark reflects on the formative years of yachting in Lymington.

Lymington had been a centre for ship and boatbuilding for centuries, so it was no surprise that yachting would take root here. In its earliest days, from around 1820, a number of wealthy owners lived in or around Lymington, and this led to the rapid growth of designing, building and racing some fairly large vessels in the vicinity. It is somewhat astonishing to learn that one early Lymington yachtsman actually sailed his vessel outside the Needles – regarded then as remarkable, not for want of either his or the boat's capabilities, but because he was nearly captured by French privateers that near to the coast.

A number of these owners were Members of the Royal Yacht Club, founded in 1815 (later the RYS) but, as their group grew, it is no wonder that they wished to get together locally, so towards the end of the 19th century, the first Lymington Yacht Club was formed. It met in the hexagonal upper room of the Bath House (now part of the LTSC Clubhouse).

The driving force behind the original LYC were Major C Fox-Roe and Capt. James Dyer; Fox-Roe was Secretary and the founding Commodore was General Sartorius (it is uncertain whether this was Reginald or his brother Euston Sartorius: both became Major Generals and, extraordinarily, both

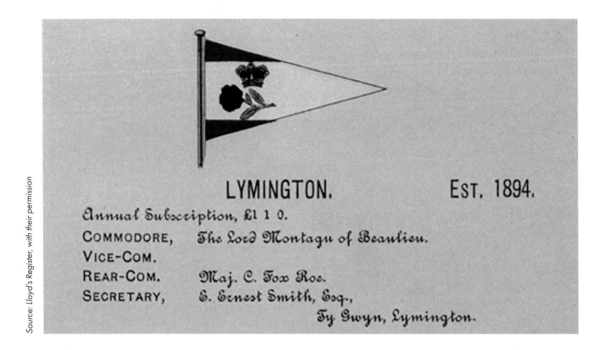

Source: Lloyd's Register, with their permission

LYMINGTON.   **EST. 1894.**

Annual Subscription, £1 1 0.
COMMODORE,   *The Lord Montagu of Beaulieu.*
VICE-COM.
REAR-COM.   *Maj. C. Fox Roe.*
SECRETARY,   *S. Ernest Smith, Esq.,*
                           Ty Gwyn, Lymington.

Evidence of the existence of the LYC in the accompanying entry in Lloyd's Register of Yachts

were awarded VCs). Evidence of the existence of the LYC, founded in 1894, is seen in the accompanying entry in *Lloyd's Register of Yachts*, showing the list of its officers and the burgee.

By 1896, the date of the Lloyd's extract, Lord Montagu had become the Commodore and Fox-Roe, Rear-Commodore. Ernest Smith was Secretary. It seems that after a few years, the fledgling LYC dwindled and was dissolved.

Next on the scene was the redoubtable Capt. H. H. (Henry) Nicholson, who, in the first years of the 20th century, brought with him from Plymouth a 14ft clinker sailing dinghy, on which the Lymington Pram Class was modelled. In order to provide some 20 or so of these boats with some organised racing, Nicholson set about forming the Lymington River Sailing Club in 1914 – not auspicious timing, given the imminent change in world affairs. Club sailing in Lymington languished after the First World War, until an energetic group, led by Major Cyril Potter, created (or more accurately, re-created) the Lymington

River Sailing Club or LRSC in 1922. That date is today taken as the origin of our Club, as it represents the start of the continuous period of Club existence.

Sadly, little else is documented of the affairs of the original LYC but we know a little more of the original LRSC: Nicholson was its Captain (it had no Commodore); Major A. O. L. Kindersley was the Hon Secretary/Treasurer;

*Capt. H. H. Nicholson
at the helm*

the Lady Member was Mrs R. L. Bayliff; and Hon. Starter, the Rev F. S. Trevor-Garrick. There may possibly have been some carry-over of Members from the 1894 Club to the first incarnation of the LRSC, 20 years later; there certainly was between the pre- and post-First World War Clubs.

Major Cyril Potter, the driving force behind the creation of the 1922 Club, features a great deal in its Centenary, but it is from this pre-history of the RLymYC that we should remember and honour Capt. Henry Nicholson, the founder of its closest antecedent. He lived in Creek Cottage near the Salterns and sailed his Lymington Pram round to the Town Quay to do his shopping. Nicholson served on the first General Committee of the LRSC and later the LYC. He was a highly respected sailor and a much-valued friend and a great help to all who indulged in that pastime.

The inscription reads: 'Presented to Capt. H. H. Nicholson by some of his yachting friends in recognition of his unfailing help and kindness to them Xmas 1927.'

Such was the regard in which he was held, that this silver salver was presented to him by fellow Club Members, whose 72 signatures it bears. This was in 1927, the year after the Club became the Lymington Yacht Club – the second LYC. The salver is to be seen today in the Club's trophy cabinet.

4 Development of the Clubhouse and Surroundings

Graham Clark, Club Historian, provides some background to the evolution of the Clubhouse and environs.

The earliest meetings of the reconstituted Lymington River Sailing Club took place in the home of Major Cyril Potter in 1922, and mark the birth of what is now the RLymYC. Potter lived in Blakes, a large house opposite the entrance to the old car-ferry slipway at the Lymington terminal. Such was his energy and drive that, in addition to holding inaugural Club meetings there, he allowed his conservatory to be used by Members on race days. However, the need for its own, permanent base was a top priority and fortunately this was satisfied by the acquisition of what was then the Admiralty Boathouse, the core structure of the current Clubhouse. A large amount of Coast Guard property in Lymington was being auctioned off, comprising: rows of cottages opposite what is now Nick Cox's chandlery; a lookout building in Captain's Row (a few doors up from the King's Head); and the boathouse.

In 1924, the boathouse was initially leased to the embryonic Club but later purchased, together with some surrounding land and foreshore, from Lymington Borough Council. Projecting from the boathouse structure was a substantial slipway. The single-storey brick structure soon became too small for the growing Club and Potter's energy again came to the fore, resulting in the creation of an upper floor, surrounded by a veranda (later enclosed) on the walls facing up, down and across the river. Access to the first floor was gained by external stairs. Members had formed a building company to pay for the development, which was fully paid off by 1928.

Energy and growth went hand-in-hand, once more, as the Club outgrew its boathouse footprint, and a two-storey brick wing was built to the north, creating the line of the front of the building we know today. This was completed in 1936, when the Club was still relatively young. Within only another two years, a further extension to the north wing was built.

The coming of the Second World War (the First having resulted in the stifling of the birth of the original Lymington River Sailing Club) caused Club activity to cease for the duration. The Club premises were requestioned for the war effort and became the base of the Auxiliary Fire Service. During that time, temporary buildings were erected on the adjacent council-owned land and were still being used some years after the war.

The single-storey Coast Guard boathouse, and the paddle steamer Solent (IV)

The Clubhouse in 1938 or 1939

Peace, and the return to normal life, saw a strong resurgence of recreational pursuits, amongst which sailing was locally a natural and key feature. The Club enjoyed another growth spurt, with modestly priced dinghies enabling many more people to enjoy the sport. The Clubhouse again rose to the occasion and, early in the 1950s, the Club's foreshore was extended to the north and riverwards. This enabled dinghies to be launched directly at high water, or down the fixed jetty to a deep-water ramp inside its pierhead berth.

The 1950s aerial photo of the Club, shown on the next page, reveals some interesting and long-forgotten features: the wartime buildings on council land to the south; the rudimentary carpark; the large dinghy storage shed to the rear; the old Thames barge *Minnedosa* amongst the Fortuna mud berths. According to reliable sources, the Club was offered the car-parking land to purchase, but the then Members were mostly brought to the Club by chauffeur and therefore did not need to park their cars. The sentry box, just beyond the dinghy shed, was for the car park attendant: neither a particularly taxing nor profitable role, one imagines. The jetty in the foreground, to the south of the Club, was under the control of the Harbour Master.

All the while, that essential of a yachtsman's life, the bar, existed at the seaward end of the ground floor, enabling thirsty crews to tumble off their boats and straight into their first pint. It was a simple affair compared to today's sophisticated setting, but it was adorned in 1947 by Douglas Wales-Smith's presentation of his magnificent painted panorama of the river, populated by so many identifiable boats and characters of their day. It can still be seen, along with its framed legend, in the Club today (*Ed. See also page 39*).

Later 20th-century development progressed, in line with growing membership, with the addition of the modern first-floor bar in 1968. As well as providing a welcome new bar, it also created new and liberated old ground-floor space for much-needed working accommodation. With this change, the old external stairs were replaced by the current internal ones, but the remnant of the iconic veranda persisted on the north wing. That, in its turn, was overtaken when the River Room was built in 1980, followed by a side extension to the north wing and the infilling the space between, providing integrated catering and service operations for the whole of the first floor.

The early 2000s saw the balcony extended; a spiral staircase to the second floor built; and ground-floor alterations made. The latter included the relocation of Doug Baverstock's boatman's workshop, from which he had kept a close eye on the waterborne activity of the Club. That enabled him, at legendary speed, to reach the end of the pontoon before any boat could berth that had the misfortune not to be flying a Club burgee.

The waterborne facilities had also changed substantially over the past 50 years. From the north end of the site, a somewhat rackety pontoon provided homes for many tenders for holders of river moorings (there were no marinas then). The fixed jetty in line with the old slipway was later shortened and the first of the current siting of pontoons was installed. These were gradually extended and transformed until the latest iteration arrived in 2015, providing what earlier sailors would have regarded as unheard-of facilities and capacity. Rather less obvious, but none-the-less relentless, was the extension and strengthening of the seawall, with the growing need to defend the site from rising water levels.

Opposite, above: Club from the air, pre-1936

Opposite, below: Aerial post war (1950s) photo from the east showing the dinghy shed

The Club from the River, evening of 2nd August 2021

Over the nearly 100 years of the Club's existence, the current site and its facilities have been the foundation of Club life, ashore and afloat. As membership has increased, so the scale and style of the Clubhouse and its surroundings has changed to meet its needs. There is every reason to expect the next century will see it flourish likewise.

It is fascinating to see the many different photos of the Club over the years. The eagle-eyed will observe the changing details, such as the copper vent on the old roof ridge; the gradual enclosing of the veranda; the brief tenure of the high-level starting box; the various means of access to the water etc. Amongst these iconic developments are included the flagstaff in its different locations, including one arrangement where its gaff is correctly facing 'aft' into the Club, as if the Club were a ship, looking ahead. From such details and the state of progress of the nearby moorings, regress of the marshes and the different passing steamers, one can date the photos that appear, though sometimes adrift from their era.

5 A Tale of Two Murals

In our Centenary year we are obliged to Brian May for sponsoring the restoration of these two wonderful murals, which are on display at the Club. Graham Clark explains their history.

Of the everyday sights in the Clubhouse, we may take for granted the two fine panoramas, painted and donated to the Club by former Members. One painting, the very large piece that for many years delighted visitors to the Island Room (formerly the Library) started off in the slipway bar, behind the bar itself. It was painted in 1947 by Douglas Wales-Smith, whose son Patrick has been a Member since 1946. The second once graced the wall behind the serving counter in the River Room, and was the work and gift of Roy Coombs in 1960.

Mural by Roy Coombs, 1960

Happily, Wales-Smith provided a key to what he called the frieze in the RLYC (sic) bar, giving us a clue to the subjects. He lists boats by class, name and owner, and reserves a special place in the foreground for Dan Bran in his dinghy. It even includes the friendly presence of the much-loved MV *Lymington*, the river's first ro-ro ferry and part of the Southern Railway's fleet.

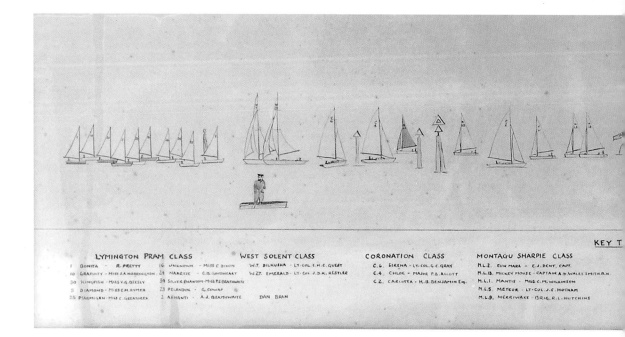

KEY T

LYMINGTON PRAM CLASS
1 BONITA - R.PRETTY
10 GRAFLITY - MISS J.A.HODBINGTON
30 KINGFISH - MISS K.G.BEESLY
5 DIAMOND - MISS C.H.RYMER
25 PTARMIGAN - MISS C.GREATOREX

16 UNKNOWN - MISS C.DIXON
29 NAARTJE - C.B.SOUTHCOTT
34 SILVER PHANTOM-MISS P.E.BRAITHWAITE
23 PELANDOK - G.COWAP
2 ASHANTI - A.J.BRAITHWAITE

WEST SOLENT CLASS
W.7 BILKUSHA - LT-COL.C.H.C.GUEST
W.27 EMERALD - LT-COL.J.D.K.RESTLER

DAN BRAN

CORONATION CLASS
C.6 SIRENA - LT-COL.G.C.GRAY
C.4 CHLOE - MAJOR P.B.ALLOTT
C.2 CARLOTTA - H.B.BENJAMIN Eq.

MONTAGU SHARPIE CLASS
M.L.2 GUN MARA - C.J.DENT, CAPT.
M.L.13 MICKEY MOUSE - CAPTAIN A.D.WALES SMITH R.N.
M.L.1 MANTIS - MISS C.M.WILKINSON
M.L.5 METEOR - LT-COL.J.C.HOTHAM
M.L.9 MERRIWAKE - BRIG.R.L.HUTCHINS

Above:
Mural by Douglas Wales-Smith – Key, 1947

Below:
Mural by Douglas Wales-Smith, 1947

Wales-Smith depicts the popular classes, both dinghies and keel-boats, as well as individual yachts, in this scene set just after the Second World War, also the Club's first Jubilee year, 25 years on from its founding in 1922. Quite rightly, the Lymington Pram Class is strongly in evidence, together with its smaller sisters, the Scows. Joining them are a good handful of Montagu Sharpies, deriving their specific name from their popularity in Beaulieu. The keel-boats are dominated by the West Solent Restricted Class and the Coronations. Also featured are a number of individual yachts, as much characters of their era as their owners.

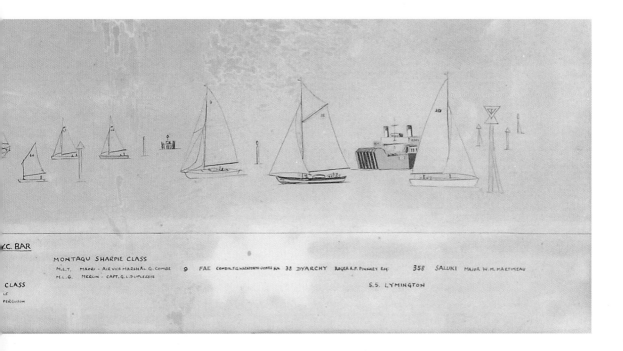

Y.C. BAR

MONTAGU SHARPIE CLASS

M.L.7.   MAORI - AIR VICE MARSHAL G. COMBE   9   FAE COMDR. F.G.MAENZORTH-JONES R.N.   38 DYARCHY   ROGER A.F. PINKNEY ESQ.   358   SALUKI   MAJOR W. M. MARTINEAU
M.L.G.   MERLIN - CAPT. G.L.DUPLESSIS   S.S. LYMINGTON

CLASS
LE
FERGUSON

And there in the background is the Club's own starting platform, given its own place in posterity.

Moving forward only 13 years is Roy Coombs' vibrant representation of racing on the river. Roy had been an active Member of the Club since 1950, sailing a range of boats and serving on committees. In his professional life he was a graphic artist, explaining the colourful and energetic treatment of the subject. With a twinkle in his eye, he once said that most Members would have an example of his work in their homes; when faced with a blank expression, he revealed that he was the artist who painted the fruit designs on Tesco's yoghurt pots!

Coombs' panorama contains fewer river features but much more by way of classes, colour and action than its predecessor, no doubt entertaining many as they queued for lunch. The piece depicts the smaller craft that flourished in the 1950s as life returned to normal but, with dinghies and open keel boats now more affordable, the sport came within the reach of many more and younger sailors. The boats featured include National 12, Firefly, Finn, GP 14 and XOD Classes, battling for supremacy in the river from in front of the RLymYC Clubhouse. Bursting with activity, the scene displays the Club's burgee, the finishing line mark and the all-important stopwatch, as well as the starting cannon and race flags, needed to set off the action. ✖

6 100 Years of Social Life

Jose Nieves, of the Club's Social Committee, writes about aspects of Club social life over the last century.

Social activities are an integral and enjoyable part of membership in a club of like-minded people. The full range of these activities has varied over the years, but for most of the Royal Lymington Yacht Club's life, the Fitting Out Party and Regatta Ball, the Annual Dinner, New Year's Eve celebrations and Winter Lecture Series (with supper afterwards) have been constants. To read the Club's social history, it does seem at times as though the success or otherwise of events has often been closely linked to the supply of alcohol, but this has been hotly disputed. As a previous Flag Officer wrote, 'Never an inkling of the Club... becoming a Drinking Luncheon Club. Sailing was the raison d'être.'

This raison d'être nevertheless always had a concomitant requirement for refreshment, which was from the very beginning properly accommodated. Founding Member Major Potter's conservatory was the original Club Room. Sometimes the Club was unable to provide: word has it that one early Steward, Mr Francis, took so long to produce any drink that the thirsty customer had time to stroll over to the Mayflower for a liquid taster before coming back to find his drink was nearly ready.

In the years before the Second World War, Members enjoyed the traditionally low-key social activities of the Club – picnics and afternoon tea. When peace returned, a bar was provided along with its requisite attendant,

Overleaf:
The years between the World Wars: families relax by the Club

who could dispense drinks immediately and willingly. Sadly there was a shortage of alcohol in 1946, although 'a benefactor' managed to obtain small but regular supplies of gin in the cold winter of 1946/47.

The scarcity of comestibles aside, Club social activities proliferated and the Grand Regatta Ball on 22 August 1947 set the standard, with Sim Grossman and his Orchestra and special catering arrangements, although this meant that the tickets were 'a little more expensive' than usual. Evening Lectures, with supper served afterwards, were a favourite social event – as they remain today.

The 1950s began with a Masked Ball, and continued to provide so many social events that Members must surely hardly ever have been home. The 1957 Bulletin thanked everyone who 'no sooner is one function over, start preparing for the next'. Older Members enjoyed Fitting Out dances, Regatta Balls, Fancy Dress Balls, Potter Ship party dinners, dances, bridge and lecture evenings, while the younger group attended junior dances and reel parties. Music lovers could enjoy afternoon gramophone recitals, and, the more energetic, Highland reels. In addition, Members could lunch at the Club more or less daily throughout the year, and suppers and teas were available during the sailing season. In between all these activities, the decade ended with a bumper crop of marriages and engagements; it was hoped that the couples would find married life a happy balance between sailing and socialising at the Club.

The 1960s started well – 'all social functions were well attended and as popular as ever' in 1960, and the 1961 season was blessed with successful 'regattas, dances, lectures etc'. However, the Club was obviously outgrowing its facilities; the hiring of a marquee for the first time, for the 1964 Regatta Ball, meant more people could attend; this was so successful that it was repeated over the following years, although there was still a maximum of 250 guests. Social life was minimal during the 1967 season when the Club was being rebuilt; however, social events re-started with a bang in 1968. The Regatta Ball was seen as a 'fitting introduction' to the rebuilt Club (even the weather behaved), and the bar, run by one Clive Fry, was regarded as 'the established centre' of the Club's social life, being so busy that there was a worry that any

Christmas is always taken very seriously at the Royal Lymington. Pottership magazine no. 18

extra takings would be eaten up by the necessity of providing more staff. By 1969, the social calendar included an Easter Regatta (followed by a discotheque), the Regatta Ball, the Annual Dinner, Wine Dinners, the New

Year's Eve Ball, the Race Game Evening and a Bridge drive.

Social events organised to commemorate the 50th Anniversary of the founding of the Club included an exhibition of artefacts and documents illustrating its history to date. All Members were given a book on the same subject, funded by donations from some of the Members, and well received by all.

During the 1970s, Club Members welcomed a series of distinguished speakers to its lecture nights and formal dinners. These included the author and sailor Hammond Innes, Antarctic explorer Sir Vivien Fuchs, architect Sir Hugh Casson and sailors Naomi James (who single-handedly sailed round the world via Cape Horn in 1978) and Chris Dunning (the 1977 Captain of the British Admiral's Cup team and a survivor of the terrible events of the 1979 Fastnet Race. On one occasion, Lord Amory (the MP), Padre Logan and Sir Dermot Boyle (Marshal of the RAF) apparently gave speeches which belied the apparent serious nature of their professions and had the guests rolling in the aisles. The usual roll of club parties, balls and dinners was augmented by other events, such as the Jubilee Bridge Drive (1972), the first of the annual art exhibitions (1975), the attendance of 180 Members at the Spithead Jubilee Review (1977) and the instigation of an annual barbeque. In 1977, this event took place on Hurst Spit in force eight to nine winds. The first Committee Members' Dinner occurred in 1978 along with the Club lottery, which was promoted with the plea

In 1995, parties were many and various. Pottership *magazine no. 14*

different arrangements for this event. One idea is to have two dinners - a Turkey Christmas Dinner and a Goose Christmas Dinner on different days but fairly close together. Reactions to this idea would be welcome.

The Theme suppers have been popular, some more than others, and we will be thinking whether to have so many next year, or whether to have some different ones. All these ideas are under constant review.

At the time of writing we await the Viennese Evening (fully booked soon after booking was opened), the Nautical Quiz and the Murder Evening.

Now it will soon be the sailing season again and we like to be on hand ashore to help with arrangements there. We are always looking for volunteers to help on occasions like the Summer Regatta and the Junior Regatta in August. Please let me know if you would be willing to help at the barbecue in the evenings of the Summer Regatta or with serving snacks on the forecourt for the Junior Regatta.

In the dining room the new tables are well in use and the table mats were popular as Christmas presents: by next winter we hope to have smart new crockery. But there are still lots of things we want to do and it is a job deciding which should come first. Rest assured - there aren't many days on which there isn't at least one House Committee Member working hard on Members' behalf.

Mary Follett
Rear Commodore House

House Partying

My first year has been busy and I can't believe it is already over. Only two more to go!

Our 'Sound of the Sixties' laying up party went well, the band being particularly successful. We are hoping to have them back for the next New Year's Eve party.

As usual, the Christmas dinner was fully booked the day booking opened, although on the day there was actually no-one on the waiting list. However, we are looking at 'we would like more gamblers please... We hope that some more Members will abandon the pools, cancel their accounts with William Hill, and invest in the Club.' It is uncertain how such a request would be received in 2022.

HRH Princess Anne was the guest of honour at the Cruising Dinner in 1980, a year which brought a round of seemingly almost ceaseless social activity which set the scene for the rest of the decade; the New Year's Eve Party of 1980 was fully booked by the beginning of November, and there were regular speciality suppers (such as the Goose Supper); 'foreign' evenings were also instigated, where a lecture was tied to an appropriate meal. The usual mixture of formal and informal dinners and events took place each year and, in the first ever *Pottership* magazine in spring 1989, the Commodore celebrated the importance of the social life to the main activities of the Club: 'In the Clubhouse... we foster the social activities which are so important in bringing together a membership with such widely varied talents and interests. We are also able, in one way or another, to "wine" and "dine" them for 363 days in the year: not a bad achievement, and one that complements the purpose of the club, "to encourage and promote yachting in all its aspects".'

By the 1990s, there was a well-established round of social events: the dinners, lectures, suppers and parties being supplemented by a weekly Club Night, designed to help Members get to know each other better. Jazz seems to have been a major source of social entertainment during the 1990s, while the less energetic were able to enjoy the forementioned 'foreign' themed suppers, the 'speciality' meals and the Christmas dinners.

The Club celebrated its 75th anniversary with 'fireworks and fizzy drinks, gunfight and fleet review, vintage dinghies and classic jets'. The firework display, from Ray and Eric Williams' barge, was so spectacular that it encouraged nine-year-old Michael Butler to write a poem, published in the autumn edition of the *Pottership*.

The new century began with a family New Year's Day Brunch. The Club was interested to know everyone's views on whether this could be a

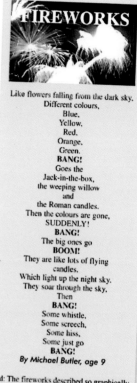

FIREWORKS

Like flowers falling from the dark sky.
Different colours,
Blue,
Yellow,
Red,
Orange,
Green.
BANG!
Goes the
Jack-in-the-box,
the weeping willow
and
the Roman candles.
Then the colours are gone,
SUDDENLY!
BANG!
The big ones go
BOOM!
They are like lots of flying
candles,
Which light up the night sky.
They soar through the sky,
Then
BANG!
Some whistle,
Some screech,
Some hiss,
Some just go
BANG!
By Michael Butler, age 9

Ed: The fireworks described so graphically here were of course the display celebrating the Club's 75th anniversary. A collection for the RNLI taken amongst the spectators outside the Club raised £120.

Michael Butler's poem and, on the next page, the anniversary celebrations which inspired it. Pottership magazine no. 19

Y CELEBRATION

much activity in the middle. Photo: Noel Hutchings

The Downton Village Band looked and sounded
impressive on the pontoon in the late afternoon.
Photo: William Payne

The principal reviewing boat was the
Commodore's *Letitia Jean*.
Photo: William Payne

grey day.
...to: Paul Rawlinson

High spirits and high hats aboard Coric.
Photo: William Payne

Centre
fascinatin

Classic boats at the pontoons aroused
great interest.
Photo: Paul Rawlinson

The fire
celebration
grand sho

This is ty in Aquayla.
William Payne

ntrance hall: the
re designed and
by Jo Burchell.

specially for the
Butler, made a
om Ray & Eric
liams' barge.
William Payne

replacement for the New Year's Eve Ball; it probably says something about the sociability of the membership that, at least when there is no pandemic raging, we now enjoy both. In the winter months of 2001, Vince Sutherland took on the task of organising the monthly quiz nights – and continues to do so today. The following year, in 2002, the Club celebrated Her Majesty The Queen's Golden Jubilee with a Jubilee Ball, a lunchtime party, a loyal toast and a 21-gun salute. The first annual photographic exhibition took place in 2007, while lecture nights and suppers, bridge and quizzes, parties and balls, Burns Nights and Valentine's evenings all ensured that the first decade of the 21st Century was enjoyed to the full at the Royal Lymington.

In 2010, the refurbished bar was described by the Commodore as 'A great place to meet friends over a pint and put the world to rights... Looking forward to another year of... activity both on the water and socially. I am confident

Her Majesty The Queen's Golden Jubilee Celebrated at the Club. Pottership magazine no. 29

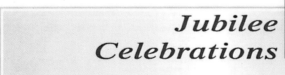

1952 | 2002 | THE QUEEN'S GOLDEN JUBILEE 2002

Jubilee Celebrations

...THE LUNCHTIME PARTY - LOYAL TOAST AND 21 GUN SALUTE

The firing party - Pat Fulton, Allan Collison, Desmond Waring, Duncan MacAlister, Alexander Kilgour, Anthony Ruffell, Mac MacDougall

Photos Mike Saunders

Before proposing the Loyal Toast the Commodore Andrew Tyrrell presented the Jack in the Basket Trophy for the most outstanding sailor under 30 in 2001, to Nick Rogers for his second place in the 470 World Championship. The Commodore said, "A Jubilee is a reflection of the past 50 years and a challenge to do better in the future. As a Club, we have benefited from the effort of those who came before us and we should leave a heritage for the next generation".

Club members watch 21 gun salute on the pontoon

Preparing to toast the Queen

Sir Ben Ainslie on the balcony of the Club after his 2012 Olympic success. Pottership magazine no. 39

the Club will retain its friendly and welcoming ambience for Members and visitors alike.' The social scene certainly lived up to expectations. There was no diminution in parties or balls, dinners or lunches, lectures and speakers. The wedding of Prince William to Catherine Middleton was celebrated with coffee, Buck's Fizz and pastries; pink champagne was served to toast the happy couple and lunch included a special Royal Wedding Souvenir Menu. The following year, 2012, the Club celebrated both Her Majesty The Queen's Diamond Jubilee and the arrival in Britain of the Summer Olympic Games. The weekend of 2/3 June saw a Queen's Diamond Jubilee hog roast followed the next day by an opportunity for Members to watch the Jubilee River Pageant on the big Club screen and to enjoy the 'Big Jubilee Buffet

Lunch with Proms-style Sing-along'; a few nights later, a supper was held at the Club to celebrate the departure from Southampton, on their Jubilee voyages, of the three Cunard Queens – *Elizabeth*, *Mary* and *Victoria*. Ben Ainslie's Olympic sailing success was celebrated when he visited Lymington shortly after his victory, and the Club thronged with Members who enjoyed a wonderful evening of celebration, with much vying to hold his gold medal.

In the years following these events, right up to the beginning of 2020, the social life at the Royal Lymington continued to thrive. Dancing lessons (the jive) provided both participants and spectators with much enjoyment, and bridge classes continued to thrive. Other activities were added to the list: yoga and Pilates, informal ladies' lunches and monthly Friday afternoon teas vied for attention with no fewer than three cycling groups, several monthly book groups and an art group. By 2019, the Royal Lymington social scene was so busy that even members of the House Social Sub Committee were sometimes surprised by what was on offer.

2020 started with such promise but the arrival of the Covid-19 pandemic to British shores led to a total national lockdown in March. However, the social activities of the Royal Lymington did not cease; they were merely adapted. We were allowed to exercise once a day; therefore, the various cycling groups continued, with a few tweaks to ensure adequate social distancing. An online weekly newsletter began on 6 April 2020, filled with news and helpful advice on subjects ranging from online photography and sailing courses to providing practical help to Members of the Club who had to isolate. The Book Club, yoga, Pilates, Bridge Club, Tuesday night lectures and art group all went online. There was a virtual regatta, rainy day photography, an online happy hour and a mini quiz, prepared and presented, as usual, by Vince. Pre-dinner virtual concerts were arranged by Phil and Katherine Collett.

Once the lockdown ended, the Club reopened and – although strict social distancing was observed at all times – it was possible to re-open the restaurant and to restart sailing. Sadly, the inexorable march of the pandemic saw another period of restrictions, so the Club promptly restored internet activities: an online cream tea in November, an online art exhibition and, at

The Royal Lymington Yacht Club manages to combine its raison d'être of sailing (the Jardine twins are among its many Olympic alumni) with social activities. Here Ado and Stewart celebrate their 80th birthday with cake at the Club after Wednesday afternoon XOD Racing in 2013

the beginning of 2021, a very enjoyable virtual Burns Night and an equally entertaining virtual Valentine's.

Sailing seems very often to go hand in hand with vibrant social activity. The excitement of the race at sea is relived in the aftermath of the event; a day of happy cruising is enhanced by drinks in the cockpit as the sun goes down. All the various aspects of sailing – the racing, the cruising, the mucking about in boats, the learning how to sail – have, can and will continue to flourish at Royal Lymington. The social events which the Club organises serve to unite these sometimes disparate interests to produce a Club membership where everyone can, if they wish, take an informed and active interest in everything that is going on. Over the years, social activities at the Club have adapted to the changing fashions and expectations of life. In 2022 there are more retired Members of the Club than ever before, and fewer teenagers and young 20s. The Club's Social Committee members are constantly seeking ways and ideas for attracting these younger age groups back to the Club, to continue to adapt and introduce the social activities which newly married Members were once encouraged to enjoy, in happy balance with the Club's raison d'être of sailing.

7 Two Notable People

Annie Littlejohn 1920–2022

One Member who was alive from the inception of the Club up to our Centenary was stalwart Annie Littlejohn, who joined the Club in 1947 and was active in all areas for most of the rest of her long life. Below are a few of the tributes paid to Annie by Club Members on the occasion of her 100th Birthday.

Annie Littlejohn

'Hello Annie would you like a gin & tonic?' 'Of course darling, make it a large one please.'
RLymYC Commodore 2012–15 Phil Lawrence

I first met Annie at the London Boat Show when she was the hostess for International Paints. We met almost daily – she was dispensing free drinks. She knew many friends from Burnham-on-Crouch. The second year of the SBS, I told her that my partners were placing our half-tonner at Lymington and she offered me hospitality at the weekends in the house where she and Sandy lived. After a while during Sunday night dinner, Sandy said that he couldn't understand why I didn't live down here, at which Annie said she would find me somewhere. I drove back to my flat in Neal Street the next morning to find a message from Annie on the answerphone. I immediately rang back and was greeted by: 'I have found you a place to live, but you must come back and see it this morning!' I did as instructed and moved in over the next week and said goodbye to the 'smoke'. Our relationship has always been at this breakneck pace and long may it continue. One hundred is just a milestone for Annie.
Bob Fisher

Annie was such a constant in our Junior Sailing lives. Always there to help and never judgemental when things went wrong, as they often did. A wonderful support and of course great fun to have around.
Jonathon and Ann Rogers

I first met Annie one evening during 1974. I was in Lymington undertaking some training with the British 420 squad prior to their Worlds. I got a call asking for help with pumping out the Littlejohn's yacht Seawitch, which was taking on water subsequent to launching. What I thought might take just an hour or two turned into an 'all-nighter' whilst the planks took on water and stopped the river from flooding the bilge. It was a long-suffering task. But the one thing that became very apparent to me and subsequently proved to be unfailing was the enduring hospitality of Annie. No matter what the

time of day or night or the circumstance, Annie was always ready with a cup of soup, sandwich, three-course meal or just a gin & tonic. Three cheers for Annie.
Ken Kershaw

Twenty years ago I met Annie at Junior Regatta. 'Darling,' she said, 'don't mention you are a DFL (down from London), people can be a bit funny.' With that, Amanda Dingwall took the two registration forms out of my hand, read them and raised her eyes to heaven – 'Oh! Not more from London!' Annie patted me on the back and said in a stage whisper – 'Offer to help.' I did and have enjoyed every moment since of volunteering at Junior Regatta.
Shireen Crowe

I remember Annie during the first days of my chef apprenticeship at the Club for Mr. Alan Brooks in 1964. I can see her now coming into the kitchen, which was self-service in those days with Sandy and Titch, who Mr. Brooks would start twirling around calling her his bumblebee. Annie (no Mrs. Littlejohn in those days!) used to sail with Titch's godfather George Senior in his boat called Bodegita. She was always an active Member of the Club and especially with the Race Committee, and always on duty every Thursday night racing. Happy Birthday Annie.
Mike Webb

Match Racing at Lymington in its heyday was a serious business, with many very important people trying to find their way on to the Committee vessel. However, control remained firmly in the grip of the formidable duo of Annie and Eileen Caulcutt. One particular day in Christchurch Bay, delays ensued waiting for the wind to arrive, which led to a degree of irritation amongst the competitors and the inevitable chatter on the VHF implying criticism of the Race Committee. Finally, racing was due to start and the pairings, identified by large letters, were displayed on the side of the Committee vessel. I was driving a RIB, paired with a well-known yachting

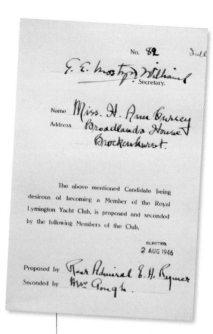

Annie Littlejohn's application to join the Club in 1947

journalist and author, and Annie certainly had us clearly marked in her naughty boy's book. Imagine our amusement when the letters DEAF were displayed, so appropriate on this important occasion. We motored close in to a restricted zone, and stood up with our ears cupped. Most on-board looked on at us perplexed. As usual though, Annie was razor-sharp and burst into laughter. But for some mysterious reason we still remained classified as naughty boys.
Nigel Brooks and the naughty boys.

I was chairman of jury at an Optimist weekend and Annie was a member of that jury. We had a rule 69 hearing to discuss bad language by a certain participant. Both helmsmen involved came in and started to present their case. I asked the protestor what words had been used and he refused to repeat them in front of Annie. Her words were classic: 'My darling, I was in the Navy and I can assure you I have heard every swear word in the book!'
Barry Dunning

Annie helped everywhere and all the time, especially during the famous Royal Lymington Cup which started in the early 70s. Since there was a weight limit involved, skippers and crew had to be weighed, which was Annie's task and only Annie's. Nobody was allowed in the weigh-in office, where all these young men stripped to their underpants anxiously waiting for the accumulative weight result, sometimes being told off by Annie. It was tricky if they were close to the limit and still had one crew to weigh in – for some this meant getting dressed in their wet suits and driving to the airport with radiators blasting hot air and the windows closed, picking up the missing crew and returning to the Club where Annie was waiting. This went on for over 20 years.
Elsa Green

Annie was a constant presence through the early years of my sailing career, always there with an encouraging hug, or pertinent anecdote. Alongside Ken Kershaw and John Doerr, her vast experience with Race and Protest

Committees created opportunities for us to develop a nuanced understanding of our sport's rules and administration during the days of the mighty 264 Lymington Cadet squadron (when Lymington held more than half of the national squad positions). These lessons served me well as I moved into the professional arena, and also when I was able to share with race management teams from the Caribbean to South Africa. I will be forever grateful to Annie for the confidence she built within me, and I am thrilled to be able to share a small part of this magnificent occasion on her 100th birthday.
Damien Dingwall

As ever, Annie puts us all in the shade! She has seen (and mostly done) everything that has happened in the Club's history. She is now one of the few who can tell us from her personal experience what VE Day felt like 75 years ago. She was the staunchest of supporters of the Navy, as well as the Club, of course. As the new Club Secretary in 2008, it took me a while to appreciate that her bark was worse than her bite – but only just.
Kevin Podger

Over a decade racing in the Royal Lymington Cup, Annie was a permanent and welcoming presence. She assisted Eileen Caulcutt in the organisation of the regattas. My abiding memory of Annie is her enthusiasm and cheerfulness at all times. On occasional subsequent visits to RLymYC when I caught up with her, she was always so pleased to chat and interested in all the crews. An absolute stalwart.
Harold Cudmore

Annie, as a General Committee Member, interviewed me when I applied for membership in 1991. I had already experienced a very formal interview with another Committee Member conducted across the large mahogany committee table in what was then the Library, so I was relieved to find that Mrs. Littlejohn wished to interview me over a G&T on the balcony.
Jane Clegg

Doug Baverstock 1927–2018

Michael Webb compiled this short piece about local character Doug Baverstock at the time of his funeral in 2018.

Douglas James Beverley Baverstock was a well-respected man who was a legendary part of Lymington River, the Western Solent, the Yacht Clubs and Lymington Lifeboat, spanning many years.

He was born at Gordleton Mill Farm on 13 November 1927, to Tom and Adeline, brother to Norman, Betty, Veronica, Marion, twins Doris and Dorothy, and Margaret. Betty, Veronica, Dorothy and Norman predeceased him, after a fishing boat accident in the Solent.

After two years at Gordleton the family moved to Ashley, Arnewood Farm, and by all accounts it was an idyllic life, with lots of space to play and roam. The farm had chickens, milking cows and arable farming, all done with horses and ploughs. Later on came the first tractor and a steam engine, towing a threshing machine. It was a different world: the grocer would call on a Thursday for the order and it was delivered Saturday, when Doug would go to New Milton, to the cinema called La Scala, and later to the Waverley after it was built.

Doug's father Tom worked for Farmer Browning alongside his two sons, but in 1936, when they moved to Lower Pennington, his calling to the sea began. He joined the Oxey Pennington Sea Scouts with a number of friends: Ted and Jack Blachford, Fred Galpin, Ray Stone, Geoff Phillips, Derek Dashwood and their Scoutmaster, who was a Mr. Bill Smith at that time.

The school was at Upper Pennington, run by Mr. Tillet, who was free with his cane, but, according to Doug, a Mrs. Torah was much nicer; school uniforms were purchased from Bennett's in Lymington. Recreation was hand-lining flounders off the seas wall, digging bait, collecting winkles and cockles, ferreting for rabbits and other such country sports.

When the time came to leave school, Doug went to work at Beesley's shipyard above the bridge at Lymington, serving his apprenticeship alongside Bob Cook during the war and gaining his shipwright's ticket. They built boats

Doug Baverstock

like 27ft Montague whalers, motorboats, tenders, dinghies and work for the
Navy, War Department and Air Force, repairing numerous small craft. They
also had the chance to go into the heavily mined Solent on delivery runs, but it
entailed getting a daily two-flag signal from Yarmouth, because up at Sowley

there was a boom laid right across the Solent with two gates; each gate formed by two ships. They got their flags and moved up to East or West Solent.

He then moved with the family in 1946 to Lymore, at Everton, where Farmer Bacon employed his father. For pleasure in 1949, Doug and two friends ferried a Lymington Scow to Le Havre and sailed the Seine to Paris; the following year they hiked from Cherbourg to Concarneau, but the Lymington River and the Solent were Doug's life and passion.

From 1950, he shared three fishing boats over the years with Arthur Renouf: there was the *Saraid*, and the *Bay Queen*, but the one I remember well was *Handy Billy*, which I saw him build and fit out at Bill Smith's boatyard on Lymington Quay. In 1951 he then went on to work at Captain Adam's Boatyard in Keyhaven.

The family then moved to Tithe Barn in 1952. In 1957, the Keyhaven Boatyard was experiencing a downturn and had to lose a shipwright; the yard's loss was the Yacht Club's gain, starting a happy association over many years, when Doug was employed by the then Sailing Secretary, Commander Brown, starting at a £7 10s wage, rising to £8 if he passed the grade, which he probably did.

Doug was 'Mr. Royal Lymington Yacht Club' personified: a jack-of-all-trades in those days, from ferrying Members, replacing oil drum pontoon floats every year, stoking the coal fires every morning in the winter, to helping in the bar with the then Secretary and wife, George and Vi Edwards.

Many Flag Officers, Members and Secretaries have gone, but I've never forgotten the encouragement, the wit, the knowledge and the caustic comments from Doug. His legacy lives on in the guise of a launch bought by the Yacht Club as a Committee Boat and named *Baverstock*, still moored at the end of the river and still being used for dinghy-racing starts and finishes.

Doug was also past chairman of the Keyhaven and Lymington Wild Fowlers Association that at one point boasted over 80 members. He also had a punt with an extremely long and heavy punt gun, which he used on Hawker's Lake, shooting duck. He later passed it on to St Barbe's Museum.

His Club workshop was the hub of the banks, with locals Harry Eales, Jack Smith, Arthur Renouf, Alf Claridge, Charlie Perriton the Customs Officer and many more often calling in for a chinwag. Doug also advised and assisted hundreds of Members during his 35 years at the RLymYC, becoming an Honorary Life Member when he retired.

In 1991 Doug bought the hull of a Falmouth gaff cutter and fitted it out at Chris Deveulle's Aquaboats, where it was launched by the then Rear Commodore Sailing, Sally Potter. I remember sailing *Ada* with him, Chris Devalue and Duncan Hall one evening, after firstly shouting at me to tie the correct bit of rigging on to a cleat. It went on to be a most memorable evening, sailing up to Hurst passing the Castle so close, you felt you could touch the beach. A pint at The Gun was followed by the most beautiful sail back, on a June evening, through the lakes and coming out at Pennington; it was unforgettable. Doug sold *Ada* in later years and bought a motor day boat, calling it *Katy May*; after it got a bit difficult for him to get in to, he sold it to his dear friend Derek Smith.

Doug's knowledge of the Western Solent area and Lymington River was legendary; he was a man who could lay a mark or buoy without any new-fangled apps or what have you, but he took a bearing from a landmark, a tree, or Sway Tower, for example, then you awaited the order to drop the anchor and it was in the right position.

In the 1960s a gentleman called George Power invited some of those original Sea Scouts of 1937 to join with him and his fleet of powerboats – which were called *Torshent*, *Seeker*, *Maid of Baltimore* and *McLannahan* – to be members of Lymington's first rescue service for Lymington River and district. There were four volunteer watches of crew, of which Doug was a founder member. The first call was at a grounded yacht off Pennington, and the rescue crew were Bill Smith, Doug Baverstock, Jack Blachford and Keith Bacon.

In 1965 the RNLI were approached to take over the inshore lifeboat rescue service for Lymington and the Western Solent; another happy time began, with Doug being a founder member of the Lymington RNLI Rescue Service. He served with the D-Class and B-Class lifeboats, as coxswain, until he retired, and remained at the station as Honorary Bosun. Doug was old school, as everyone here knows, but his advice and encouragement to new crew, many of whom were related to him, was always listened to.

Doug was also the force behind the annual Sprat Suppers held at the Masonic Hall, where, in 1981, 197 diners consumed 9 stone of sprats. I remember that well, as I cooked them, but £200 was raised for the local Fisherman's Association and the RNLI, a fairly hefty sum in those days.

Doug advised the Members and he admonished them as well. He could be an acerbic commentator on the waterfront and would have the ability to strip away pretension and puncture pomposity with a few well-chosen words. A tale goes that one day a Member was having a frustrating afternoon, trying to get his boat alongside, and with each pass found it increasingly unlikely to succeed, until a lull in the wind came and the unmistakable Hampshire lilt came over: 'Tell you what sir, you stay right there and I'll bring the pontoon over to you.'

One aspect of his caring nature was recounted to me by Alan Coster. One day, Alan and Malcolm Smith borrowed a sailing boat and sailed over to Yarmouth. By all accounts, and not unsurprisingly after a few jars, they were drunk. It was a balmy evening with no wind, and on the way back in the darkness, the boys were forced to row the dinghy back to Lymington. Doug must have been concerned as they encountered him at the Platform; after he'd ascertained they were alright, they then asked for a tow back into port and received the answer: "NO, you got yourself in the mess, carry on as you were doing." – and then he left them.

Doug had many encounters with the Patron of the Yacht Club, the Princess Royal, taking her out in the Club launch to various yachts during regattas, and memorably ferrying her and Commander Lawrence, as he then was, to their yacht on the trots, opposite the band stand, so avoiding the paparazzi who had camped out there and who never got a picture.

In 1990 Doug was so pleased to receive the BEM for services to the community and the Yacht Club. He retired in 1992 and lived with his sister Margaret, still enjoying life, going out in Katy May, having a few drinks with friends on the pontoon, and in later years, still coming down to the banks in his new vehicle – an electric buggy – although I am sure he was a safer driver on the water. ⚓

8 The Club's Silver Jubilee – 1947

Graham Clark, our Club Historian, looks back at the Club's Silver Jubilee celebrations in 1947.

The Club is currently celebrating its Centenary Year but what of previous celebrations, to mark its Jubilees, every quarter-century? Many Members will remember the 75th, in 1997, and a few will recall our Golden Jubilee in 1972 but very few indeed would have been Members as long ago as the Silver, in 1947.

In those post-war, grey days of reconstruction, rationing, shortages of materials and products, the ability to get onto the water – as cheaply as possible – must have been a Godsend. The heavy snowfall early in that year gave way to a blistering summer, followed by the happy event of the wedding of HRH Princess Elizabeth to Lt Philip Mountbatten, RN.

The Club had only existed for 17 years when it had to be shut down at the outbreak of war, with the Auxiliary Fire Service taking over the building. So, it is not surprising that the joyful resurgence of Club life, after victory and peace, would have preoccupied Members, rather than considering celebrations in a time of austerity, of a rather young milestone of 25 years, during six of which the Club was closed.

There are few photos of Members' doings or of events from that time – the few offerings include these images of the small Club Handbook of those days:

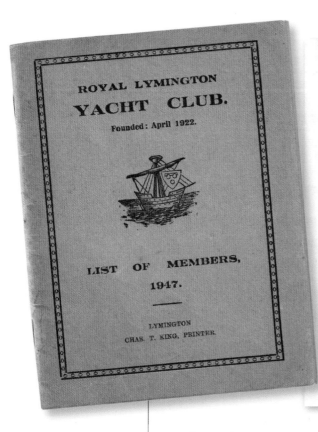

... from which it may be noted that this copy was that of the Vice-Commodore, Major Bill Martineau (he went on to become Commodore in 1954). The inner page, listing the Club Officers, reveals a preponderance of military ranks and decorations, reflecting the era recently passed.

The previous year, the Club's first post-war season, had seen the resurgence of class and handicap racing. Post-war restrictions were easing and allowed more extensive cruising – the extremes of Sweden to the north and Biscay to the south must have seemed exotic in their day. The Club programme included lectures, notable amongst which were famous names such as Humphrey Barton, who went on to cross the Atlantic in his Laurent Giles designed 25ft *Vertue XXXV* (her painting and his Rear-Commodore's framed burgee still adorn the Clubhouse (he went on to found the Ocean Cruising Club). Barton was joined on the lecture list by no lesser names than Eric Hiscock, Major 'Blondie' Hasler RM, and Charles Currey, cousin of the Club's doyenne, Annie Littlejohn.

There were occasional dances, despite shortages of alcohol, and a caterer was appointed. The character of the Club was very much one of Members' self-help, including transforming the building and its facilities. Such voluntary effort even ran to deputising for the Club barman when he went on holiday.

Racing started and finished mostly at the Clubhouse, so was more of a spectator sport than today. A Regatta Fund was created to help pay for that

Here is depicted, in true atmospheric style, the Commodore during the 25th year of the Club: Col. The Hon. C. H. C. Guest in 1947

aspect of Club activity, including an anonymous collection box for contributions, which was placed strategically near the bar.

Membership had increased steadily after the war: the re-starting of Club activity in 1946 had already attracted an increase in membership to over 450, rising further to 522 in 1947 – the target was to reach a stable level of around 800 Members, with an emphasis on Members who would cherish and maintain the atmosphere of the Club, despite its growth in numbers. Different times but similar issues: the general aim was 'to extend facilities equally to all sections of its membership, so that everyone is given a good return for his or her subscription'.

The Clubhouse, still with a wartime building on the south apron

It is interesting to examine the demography of the membership in 1947 and to consider how this established the Club's character. Of the 389 Full Members and 133 Family Members, nearly three-quarters were local – i.e. they lived near enough to come down for a drink at lunchtime or for an evening's racing. Many of those listed as Full Members were in fact spouses of Full Members; presumably those designated as Family were those less active on the water.

One dramatic factor is that, breaking down the membership by date of joining, over 40 per cent of Full Members joined after the war (1945–47), whilst Family Members joining post-war made up nearly 80 per cent of that

category. Of the longer-standing Full Members who were part of the Club from 1922 to 1939, 23 were Original Members and 25 Life Members (it is not recorded how Life Membership was defined). 176 Full Members joined in the 1930s. It is unclear if any Members ceased their membership at the outbreak of war and were counted amongst the post-war influx if they then re-joined.

The Flag Officers and Committee were keeping a special eye on the Town River Committee (under the control of the borough council) and its negotiations with the Southern Railway company, whose ferries plied the route to Yarmouth. The first double-ender car ferry, the MV *Lymington*, had arrived in 1938 with a capacity of 20 cars; it was about to be joined by a similar vessel, the diesel-electric paddle vessel *Farringford*, capable of embarking 30 cars.

Afloat, most Members' boats were on river moorings, accessible by owners' dinghies, including many heavy dinghies; some sailing dinghies were housed on the Club's forecourt. Wherever their boat was moored, all Members would have met passing through the Club, with its waterside facilities as the main focus. Conviviality amongst a small sized membership would have been the order of the day. Returning ashore, the Club bar on the ground floor – immediately in front of the Club jetty –

would have been the natural point of return (or should that be of no return?) where the day's adventures would have been re-lived, tricky anchoring stories exchanged or close-fought battles dissected minutely.

Of other aspects of the Club: a third storey was being contemplated; a new category of Cadet Member was introduced allowing young people (whose parents were not Members) to join without having to pay an entry fee); an additional summer boatman was recruited; and the three Club-owned Lymington Prams were much in demand amongst Members. The only gesture towards a special celebration was the Grand Regatta Ball, with a live band and special, high-standard catering.

All in all, this sounds like business as usual, rather than a celebration of 25 years of Club existence, with Members keen to get about their sailing activities. It was the next 25 years that were to see the major growth and establishment of the Club's character. ✖

9 Berthon and the Royal Lymington Yacht Club

Brian May writes about the entwined history of Berthon Boat Company and the Royal Lymington Yacht Club – long-time friends and neighbours on the Lymington River.

The Royal Lymington Yacht Club's legacy in Lymington is interwoven with Berthon's, both river stakeholders embracing the Solent and oceans beyond, creating modern means to tempt locals' interest in being afloat, and providing a haven for yachts ashore and afloat, thereby creating a tapestry of past and present. The two take pride in the impressive shared heritage on the river frontage, sewn into a combined storyline.

The Reverend Berthon and his Collapsible Boat

In 1841, Reverend Edward Lyon Berthon entered Magdalene College to study theology and in 1845 he was ordained as a curate of Lymington. His new coastal location allowed him to indulge his passion for nautical invention: in particular the idea for which he is most recognised, the Berthon Collapsible Lifeboat.

The ingenious design was a response to one of his clergymen, Reverend Clark, surviving the shipping disaster of PS (paddle steamer) *Orion*, which sank on 18th June 1850, drowning 41 out of the 200 souls on board. Berthon soon began designing and building a prototype of the collapsible lifeboat.

Berthon's, 1930s, in a photo taken by Aero Pictorial. Berthon's build shed, the slipway and adjacent smaller dinghy storage shed named 'the fridge' (owing to the bitterly cold winter easterlies), were built in 1928

Large Berthon Collapsible [Life] Boat

The portable design would be made from waterproof canvas stretched over 14 feet of hinged timber and quality-tested by allowing armies of ants and termites loose on the flax-based fabric previously soaked in a concoction of turpentine, soap, linseed oil and paint.

Berthon to May Family

Harry May, born in the West Country was formerly a boat builder on the Thames at Chertsey, then at Hammersmith where he built International 14s with fellow dinghy-racing competitor Frank Morgan Giles under the name Morgan Giles & May. With an office on the Strand, Giles and May soon saw forward orders growing to £20,000, and this necessitated moving the business to Hythe on Southampton Water; having built 6-metre yachts there, the pair were instrumental in building the early Felixstowe hydro/seaplanes. In due course, Giles left for Teignmouth where his Morgan Giles boatyard flourished.

Harry's brother Frank Aubrey May, having been wounded in the trenches and invalided out of the army due to the loss of an arm and a shattered kneecap, then joined his brother in Hythe along with new partner Mr Harden, all now trading under the banner of May, Harden & May.

The demise of Edward Berthon junior provided Frank May with an opportunity, acting as nominee for his brother George (then a USA resident and first senior partner of Price Waterhouse in the USA) to purchase the Berthon Boat Company Ltd. (George May wrote a number of books, including *Financial Dynamics*, describing the need for depreciation relief in the accounting world.) As a shareholder George would often take the *Queen Mary* across the Atlantic to visit his family and write the odd five-figure cheque to keep his siblings' heads above the waterline in its early years! Meanwhile, Harry May bought The Shipyard, named Courtney's in 1918. Merging the two entities on the Lymington River frontage under the Berthon banner, Harry and Frank developed a diverse business of yacht and commercial boat building, repairs and mud berths.

The Lymington Scows

By 1921, the Berthon Boat Company was advertising a Lymington Scow complete for £40. The *Yachting Monthly* reported it had 'standardised the model and designed elaborate jigs so that all parts may be machined and

Scows sitting ashore adjacent to the Fortuna shed with Lymington Laundry in the background

prepared for erection'; it was planked with wych elm and larch, using pine thwarts. The iron fittings were galvanised. There was also a 'de luxe' model in mahogany with gun metal fittings costing £10 more. By 1948, Berthon had produced over 200 Scows, many built for Royal Lymington Yacht Club members.

The West Solent One Design

Harry May conceived his restricted one-design class to commemorate the new Royal Lymington Yacht Club, building five in 1923 for Club Members. These were *Sapphire, Dinah, Arrow, Fenella* and *Poppette*. Names and sail numbers have changed over the years. An additional five were ordered and

W-8 Dinah

shipped to the Argentine Yacht Club, two of which are currently in restoration (2022) in Argentina.

The 'W' Boats were one of the first production racers and, according to Berthon's promotional literature, laid down in batches. A very complete and carefully made set of moulds, jigs and templates enabled them to produce these standard hulls with exceptional uniformity at a cost little more than half that of designing and building individual boats of similar size and type. In 1927 the cost delivered afloat at Lymington was £600; a six-metre at that time cost around £1,500. Only 35 of the West Solent Restricted Class (originally sold as Lymington One Design and latterly as West Solent One Design) were built, and are regarded as 'real gentlemen's yachts', although perhaps 'affordable' would have been a better description.

Although built in accordance with Lloyds requirements for small cruising yachts of those dimensions, they were essentially knockabout racing boats. Originally, they were composite built, and had two bent timbers of rock elm between a pair of oak sawn frames (spaced every 23 inches). Wrought iron floors were strapped on the frames. The planking was red pine, and 39 hundredweight of lead hung on an English elm keel. The deck was tongue and groove pine covered with canvas, teak being heavier, more expensive and the canvas covers prevented leaks!

Dinah, built in 1925, carried W-8 on the mainsail and features in many photographed race fleets. Her coach roof was heightened for a cruise around Britain in 1953, painstakingly written up by owner Peter Heaten. Brian May, Berthon's current co-owner, acquired W-8 in 2013 to train shipwright apprentices, giving them the opportunity to learn both traditional as well as modern woven fibre skills. Rather than using grown oak, new frames are laminated iroko, and the original pitch pine with canvas deck is replaced with 6mm teak deck over yellow cedar, the latter lightweight wood also used for hull planking, splined above the water line and caulked below. Club Member Brian looks forward to sailing her in the near future, especially since her centenary is fast approaching.

The Gauntlets

The next symbiotic relationship between Berthon and the Club occurred in 1934 with the 36ft 9in 12-ton *Gauntlet*, the result of an enquiry for a yacht by a Mr Berge; however, he decided on a different design built by Phillips of Dartmouth. Harry May was so incensed by this that he built his design anyway and challenged the Phillips boat to a race. By 'throwing down the gauntlet' and winning the race handsomely, this now famous design was born with much support from various RLymYC members.

W-8 Ripple (ex-Dinah) currently being completely restored (reconstructed frame by frame) at Berthon, teaching apprentices traditional as well as modern skills

Close WSODs finish off the Clubhouse
by Charles Pears

Left, above, below and overleaf: Early advertising

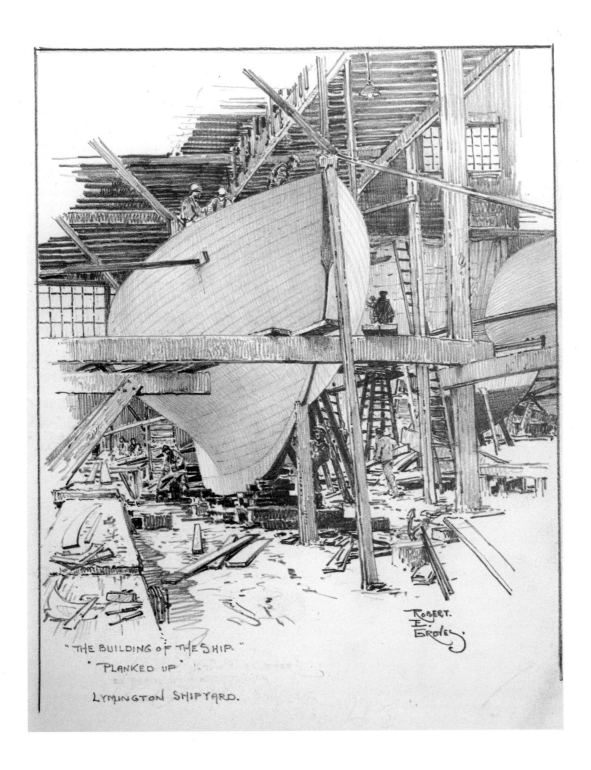

"THE BUILDING OF THE SHIP."
"PLANKED UP"
LYMINGTON SHIPYARD.

ROBERT. E. GROVES.

World War II

Between 1939 and 1945, the MOD commissioned Berthon to build 215 boats, including a variety of 72ft Minesweepers, 72ft Harbour Defence Motor Launches (HDMLs, for which Berthon became specialists), Motor Fishing Vessels (MFVs) for undercover work, and Assault Landing Craft – at record pace. Despite the international crisis, the yard produced boat after boat for the Admiralty. Many of Berthon's current staff's grandparents were employed by The Shipyard during this time, with generations of boat-builders to be found in the local area.

Post-War Period

During the war leisure boating was not allowed and boats were laid up on rivers and creeks throughout the country. After the war Lymington local, Major

Sawmill, spar shop and joiners' shop destroyed and Seaforth House damaged on 26 June 1942

Harry May, 'White Annie' and her mother Joyce Norrington

W. (Bill) M. Martineau, (who became Club Commodore later in 1954), was the first to place an order for *Saluki* in 1945, the first 14-ton Gauntlet as seen in the bottom right-hand corner of the Wales-Smith panorama. H.D. Brown followed swiftly, ordering the same and launched in 1946. Joining him in 1946 was a family order for a 14ft Pram named Gratuity for Miss Annie

Harry May (known as 'Puffer')

Norrington, living with her mother 'Auntie Jo' Joyce Norrington at Ferry House across the river. The Wales-Smith panorama has her in the bottom left-hand corner along with R. Pretty, the young boy featured in the recent Sutton Hoo find film, *The Dig*.

The Norringtons were avid supporters of the Club, and as cousins of the Mays also had shares in Berthon. Young Miss Anne Norrington was nicknamed 'White Annie' in order to distinguish her from her best and sailing friend 'Black Annie' – later Ann Littlejohn. Brian May held numerous positions at the Club with Black Annie, nicknaming her 'Mrs Bossy Yellow Boots', due to her strict control of slipway launching during the 1970s.

Being 'trade' all his life and handing over the reins of the company as his health deteriorated, Harry was delighted to join the RLymYC in 1949. Nicknamed 'Puffer', he died in 1952 at the ripe old age of 79, despite the constant roll-up between his fingers or hanging from his lip. As Harry May's son John Oliver preferred banking, John Tew became General Manager for the family shareholders, building a number of 40ft pilot service launches for the British Tanker Company (Kuwait Oil) and 100ft composite and all-wood Inshore Minesweepers and six Admiralty 42ft fleet craft Storing Tenders.

In 1958, just before David May took control of The Shipyard in 1960, Berthon built him and Jack Bryans (Club Commodore, 1958–1963) the first two of sixteen Finn Class racing dinghies; David's was named *Finnegan's Wake* (yes, clever choice); Jack's was *Definition*.

Long standing Club Member Jack Bryans ordered *Cheemaun*, launched in 1966, just in time for a mooring in Berthon's new Lymington Marina. Jack was a canny businessman and one day he came for lunch at Shipyard House and handed me a plastic yellow toy Shell tanker. Looking out of the window at the Cory Oil depot to the north he said, 'Young man, perhaps you could tell your father he should consider buying the Shell depot and turning it into a garden.' The rest is history, with the Council using its compulsory purchasing to buy two-thirds of the property to create the Town Quay car park and public conveniences in the early 1970s.

Jack's comments mentioning the Club in the mid-1960s were also in Berthon's new marketing pamphlet:

On and off since 1929 and continuously for the past 18 years I have kept my boat at Berthon Boat Company. I use them because I have been a member of the Royal Lymington Yacht Club since 1931. They have refitted my yacht

David May sailing Finnegan's Wake, built by Berthon in 1959

Cheemaun during the ten years in which I was a flag of that Club. It is due to the greatly improved quality of their workmanship, which has resulted in orders for both home and overseas markets during recent years, and my close association with the neighbourhood, that I decided to place my order for the new Cheemaun with Berthon [52ft 6in MY, launched February 1966].

David May became Managing Director at 24 in 1959 having trained as a naval architect at J.I. Thornycroft's Shipyard and Southampton University, and the following year he married Baroness Catherine Van den Branden de Reeth, whom he had met through Neil and Joan Watson, long-term Members of the Club. David set about modernising the business. David's fellow naval architect student Peter Nicholson joined Camper & Nicholson alongside his brother George. With C&N having boatyards at Southampton and Gosport, and David having Berthon at Lymington, David and Peter soon became friends and allies in promoting British yachting all around the world.

Peter married a Lymington girl, Tessa Clarke, whose father S.R.H. Clarke was an eminent racer with his *Quiver*-named yachts. He became Club Commodore in 1968/9. *Quiver II*, a 41ft 9in waterline auxiliary sloop, was launched from Berthon in 1959.

Berthon Shipyard viewed from the river in the late 60s

THE

"O.K. DINGHY"

THE FAST GROWING CLASS OF SINGLE-HANDED RACING BOATS

Designed by Knud Olsen

and sponsored by the Danish Sailing Association

and with the same characteristics as its larger sister The INTERNATIONAL OLYMPIC "FINN."

Creagh-Osborne sailing the Berthon built prototype at Lymington

BERTHON BOAT COMPANY - LYMINGTON - HANTS

71 O.K. Dinghies built by Berthon

During the 1960s, a plethora of small boats such as 71 O.K. racing dinghies were built alongside Finns, Cadets and Folkboats, whilst one-off commissions continued for larger yachts. Commodore Maj General C.W. Woods (1980–1983) commissioned a Hustler 35 fitted out at Berthon in 1972. David May's first two racing yachts were Nicholson 43s with the GRP hulls moulded by Tylers and fitted out by Berthon. The second won almost every trophy in the Solent, often racing from Lymington. Like his grandfather, he went on to build a boat a year during the decade, culminating with *Winsome Gold*, the masthead version of Ed Dubois' 7/8th rig *Police Car* (1979).

The Current Generation

David May's sons Brian and Dominic took over in 1990 and consider themselves tenants for the next generation. Brian sailed a Mirror dinghy and attended many camping adventures with the Club on the Solent north shore, Hurst Castle and Newtown Creek before sailing a few regattas in *Breathalazer* – the cockpit of which is still used to keep beer and wine cool at BBQs! Dominic raced locally in J24s and Etchells, and subsequently acquired X18, originally built by Berthon in 1924; Berthon apprentices then rebuilt her in 1992/3, competing in all RLymYC's XOD racing calendar and Cowes Week.

*Opposite:
Olympic Helmsman
R.H. Creagh-Osborne
(Club Member)*

*Winsome II
(Nicholson 43 hull,
fitted out at Berthon)
was built in 1970,
pictured with David
May at the helm;
crew includes
William Andreae-
Jones, Nicholas
Edmiston, Johnny
Urquhart (foredeck
& Berthon rigger
foreman). It was his
most successful
racing yacht, winning
most races and
regattas that year*

Meanwhile, Brian created the Berthon Source Regattas under the auspices of the RLymYC; the decade-long events attracted Admiral's Cup and Commodore's Cup race boats from all over the world to practice in the tidal waters of the Solent, enabling local boats to race with the world's best sailors. RLymYC Members manned race-officer and mark-laying vessels. International judges, including Club Members, were on-hand to police protests emanating out of multiple daily races.

The fashion for single-point lift dry-sailed race boats has morphed throughout the last 30 years to include J24, Etchells, RS Elite, Melges 24, SB3 and Folkboat classes. The current fleet of J80s compete in the Western Solent from their Berthon base on Thursday evenings and weekend racing across the year. Jointly hosted national championships included the J24, Etchells, RS Elite, Folkboat and J80 classes, and in 2001 the Etchells world championships. In all regattas, Berthon provides the infrastructure of ashore storage, craneage and berthing, with the RLymYC providing race management, clubhouse and social events. Berthon also now provides free trailer storage predominantly during weekend dinghy regattas, and permits competitors to overnight in motor-homes (as 'marina visitors') during dinghy events.

Dominic's four children George (17), Freddie (15), Henry (14) and Matilda (12) have all trained at the RLymYC over the last 10 years, with all four racing actively locally, nationwide and Europe-wide, originally in the Optimist fleet, and now in Fevas and 29ers, including European and world championships. Berthon-built Gemini RIBs are regularly deployed as safety boats driven by keen RLymYC volunteers. Berthon and the May family continue to cement the future of yachting and motor boating in Lymington. ⊗

10 Classes We Used to Sail – Dinghies

How it all began – Graham Clark looks back at popular classes sailed over the last century – starting with Dinghies...

It all began with a few Members who wanted to race their Lymington Pram 14ft dinghies and the more widely sailed Solent Seabird 18 footers, together with a handicap class for other boats. From those origins, sailing and, more specifically, racing, grew. Over the years, faster, smaller and more affordable boats meant that sailing was taken up by a wider group of Members. Alongside the dinghies, keel boats formed a strong and enduring core of both Club racing and cruising. Classes still extant are

Capt. H. H. Nicholson in the first Lymington Pram

*Lymington Prams
on the river*

dealt with on other pages, notably the XOD and the Lymington Scow both of which go back to the origins of the Club.

Early popular boats raced

Amongst classes popular with the Club in years gone by are some that are scarcely seen today. Others that have been superseded in their popularity are nevertheless still sailed widely, including the National 12, Firefly and Finn Classes. Perhaps deserving of mention, above all, is the Lymington Pram: these dinghies formed the backbone of the Club for nearly 50 years. They epitomised why the Club was formed and defined its nature; the boats were raced but were also the everyday boats of Members, who would take part in pursuit races to pleasant and (at that time) deserted anchorages, where picnics would be had; convivial gatherings and cruises were equally as important as river racing. The white yachting cap seemed to have been obligatory! Large numbers of Prams were still being sailed into the 1960s but, as some drifted their moorings more towards Keyhaven, the fleet split up and class racing diminished – it did not even feature in the Centenary of the Town Regatta, in 1975.

Planing Boats

Perhaps the most significant developments in the Club's dinghy racing are the lighter, classes of planing boats, through which Members have progressed into today's dinghies that are campaigned internationally. Thereby hangs both the stimulus and the decline of some classes within the Club. The smaller craft were affordable and provided exciting sailing; they could easily be transported to meets elsewhere, and the demand for both home and away

Firefly F1

competitions encouraged their growth in numbers while depleting the numbers racing at home. Within the Club, some notable sailing celebrities have emerged and gone on to great things. That success also had its drawbacks – imagine trailing the same superb helmsmen and crew, week after week – but then as those paragons of success found their sailing further afield, with national and international competitions – so, the home-based classes declined. Nevertheless, as the racing stars progressed, they would go up a class and introduce a new design to the Club, which then took root as other Members acquired them and benefited from the high-class competition.

Before the Second World War – the Montagu Sharpie

Dinghy racing pre-Second World War, other than the Prams or Scows, mostly featured the Montagu Sharpie, a 16ft, heavy, carvel-built boat, originating from Elkins' yard in Christchurch. The Montagu attribution arose from the class being commissioned for use on the Beaulieu River. Like the Prams, they were moored on the river during the season, there being plenty of space for boats to swing to a buoy in those days. Their heyday continued post war and a number could be seen moored well into the 1950s. Having names that began with an M, the class included *Micawber*, which was run down by the car ferry *Farringford*, but happily both crew members survived the ordeal.

Montagu Sharpie ("Mickey Mouse") helmed by Pat Wales-Smith – currently longest standing Club member – 1946. Crewed by Douglas Wales-Smith (father, and painter of Island Room mural)

National 12

The 50s and Uffa Fox

1950 saw the first mention of the Club having Fairey Firefly dinghies, along with the similarly sized National 12: both were lightweight and designed by Uffa Fox. The N12 had existed before the war, as a cheaper development of the International 14, and of simple clinker construction. Having designed

Above and below:
Finn Class

what was originally called the Sea Swallow Class, the name was changed to Firefly when Uffa was asked by Charles Currey (cousin of Annie Littlejohn), who had joined the Fairey Marine company in 1946, to supply a design that the company could build using its hot moulded ply process. Despite being similar in characteristics, both classes flourished at the Club well into the 1970s. In 1953, there was a large, low shed erected on what is now the car park, in which Nationals and other dinghies were stored. Some dinghies were also pulled up onto the concrete forecourt of the Club, where they had easy access to the water.

Members develop their racing skills and progress their boats

As the years went by, classes ebbed and flowed, as references in the Club's bulletin reveal. The Finn class was an example of how Members progressed up the dinghy ladder to compete internationally, including in the Olympics. It flourished in the 1950s but, despite being a single-hander, of simple construction and rig, it was in decline by the next decade.

Perhaps taking over the popularity of the Lymington Pram, the Club adopted the GP14 in 1960, providing both racing and family sailing like its ancient predecessor. As the 1960s progressed, Finns still made the odd appearance and the N12 fleet weakened but the Fireflies went on in strength. An interesting development around this time was that younger Members were facing challenges with life, either as students or in forging their careers; this had an impact on race attendance.

GP14

The 60s and classes change popularity

As the 1960s wore on, the not entirely unique situation arose whereby the GP14 was in decline, yet were eclipsed by their predecessors, the Prams, which still existed in some numbers. At an Easter Regatta in 1963, of the 130 boats participating, 40 were Fireflies and another 40 were Prams – ancient

420s

and modern alongside one another. Time was marching on for the Prams, however, and they were seen more on organised cruises than at class racing. Similarly, although declining in numbers racing, a fair number of GP 14s were still sailed individually.

The rise of the 420s

The late 1960s saw the emergence of classes favoured by the young: notably the Moths, Cadets, Scows, OKs and 420s – quite an eclectic mix. By the end of the decade, the 420 had been adopted as a Club class, yet there was a further fading of more general class racing, as international and open meets attracted participation. This tendency was later to be addressed by a dedicated racing strategy and the introduction of Thursday Night Racing and other regular fixtures. ⚓

11 Classes We Used to Sail – Keelboats

Graham Clark considers the keelboats sailed by Club Members over the last century.

Solent Sunbeams

The Solent Sunbeam

Of course, the Club was started by Members who already possessed some substantial keel boats, more suitable for cruising than racing, although one of the reasons the Club was created was with racing in mind. As the Club grew and a wider range of folk joined, the taste in yachts broadened. An early class that was popular around the Solent was the Solent Sunbeam, an open decked 26-footer. Designed by Alfred Westmacott, it resembles his other creations of the XOD and YOD, but possesses an extended counter stern and protruding bow. The Sunbeams were Bermudian rigged from the outset, unlike the originally gaff-rigged X. All 39 boats were built at Woodnutt's at St Helens, IOW and they were identified by their V emblem on the sail.

YACHTS ON THE RIVER LYMINGTON.

The West Solent Restricted ... and a novel feature emerges

Smaller sailing cruisers (in the 25–35ft bracket) were desired, capable of river racing as well as longer distance passage making. Early amongst these, alongside the ubiquitous, open-decked XOD, were the West Solent Restricted Class. Designed in 1924 by H. Jacobs and H. G. May (who bought the Berthon Boat Company and brought it to Lymington), five boats were commissioned by Members of the then LYC, each with a paid hand.

A novelty possessed by the WS Class was a WC! This was a source of comfort but also derision, as the vessels were greeted in local ports with appropriate 'chain-pulling' gestures!

The class extended to 27 boats but faded as the depression of the 1930s took hold. Fleets were based elsewhere including Burnham and Torbay, where the W-Class emblem was modified as WB and WT respectively.

Cruiser Racing and the Lymington L and Vertue Classes

Cruiser racing really took hold before the Second World War, and again, the echo of picnicking, as well as racing, reflected the Club ethos. This was first satisfied in the Laurent Giles-designed 'L' Class of four tonner. A more affordable yacht, the Ls, grew in number and were built locally; they went on to supplant the WS Class, dispensing with the need for paid hands. At just over 23ft long, the Ls were of a classic Laurent Giles style, and went on to develop into the Vertue Class. These were still only 25ft, but

West Solent Restricted Class, sailing in the river opposite Fortuna dock, 1930s

Lymington L Class

went on to distinguish themselves –
and the Club – with Humphrey
Barton's crossing of the Atlantic.
Back in the river, there was
increasingly intensive racing of the
Ls, about which, enigmatically,
there is a reference in the Club
archives of a racing cause célèbre
that could have led to a public
scandal had the war not intervened.
The cause? An allegation of a paid
skipper giving the owner in question
an advantage. Cheating? Amongst
gentlemen of the Royal Lymington?
Surely not!

Vertue Class

Economical racing – the Coronation Class

If there was controversy and un-
gentlemanliness surrounding L-Class racing, then the evolution of a different
class with a higher ethos may have been the result. This was to be the
Coronation Class, which arrived in that eponymous year of 1937. At only
22ft long and built at modest cost on the Clyde, they were much criticised
when they arrived in Lymington, probably by those with deeper pockets. The
boats survived longer than their allegedly cheap build predicted (some for
more than 80 years), but their Lymington owners transferred their loyalties to
the XOD, whose ranks they strengthened.

Larger yachts for Cruiser Racing – the Gauntlet Class

The Gauntlet Class represented a step up for the cruiser-offshore racer, again
from Berthon and H. G. May's drawing board. These originally 12, later 14
tonners were very sound, quick and comfortable vessels, as might be
expected of a 41ft yacht; they had a canoe stern and justified their aim of

Coronation Class

Gauntlet Class

offshore potential. The first vessel of the class appeared in 1934 and a number were acquired by Club Members. The larger version was created just before the war; the first post-war build was acquired by Major Bill Martineau MC, who went on to be Commodore some years later. The Members who owned Gauntlets, with their offshore cruising appetites, were said to be a breed apart within the Club, and took themselves off when irritations like regattas intervened! ⚓

12 Dan Bran and the Lymington River Scow

Gordon Stredwick, historian of the Scow division, provides a brief history of the evolution and rise to prominence of the Lymington River Scow.

The story of the Lymington Scow, the forerunner of the Lymington River Scow, and indeed the story of the Scow type of sailing dinghy in the UK, starts with 'a striking and bizarre character who drank like a fish' named Dan Bran.

Dan was born in Waterford, Lymington, in 1868 and inherited his father's love of boats. His father, George 'Monsey' Bran, was a fisherman who served in the crews of such famous yachts as the *Alarm*, the *Australia* and the *Fortuna*. Dan was apprenticed in the Lymington Shipyard (today the Berthon Boat Company) and then went to Poole for some years as a spar maker. He returned to Lymington in 1910 and started building on his own in a wooden shed beside the sea-water baths. He could neither read nor write but 'was a marvellous boat builder' and 'a craftsman who relied almost entirely on "eye". He had no drawings, but a wonderful eye for the lines of a boat.'*

The origin of the Scow is thought to be a Plymouth Sound Pram, sailed by Captain H. H. Nicholson on the Lymington River and Solent around 1905. The boat did not fare well in the Solent chop and was prone to

*The quotations below were published in Jean Chitty's book *The River Is Within Us*, 1983, self-published, ISBN 0-9505869-1-9. The first ('a striking...') was by Roger Pinckney (p 88 of the book), RLymYC member & past Commodore of the Royal Cruising Club. The second ('a marvellous...') was by Patrick Beesly (p 130), the author (scow owner in 1926 or 1927; his father was the well-known RLymYC member, Gerald Beesly). The third ('a craftsman...') was unattributed in Jean's book).

Above:
Captain Nicholson

Below:
The Captain in
his Plymouth
Sound Pram

stopping. Captain Nicholson wanted a more sea-friendly design and in 1912 he commissioned Dan Bran to design and build an 11ft Pram (which later became known as the Lymington Scow) at a cost of £20. The Lymington section of the *Cruising Association Bulletin* reported in January 1913 that 'Bran, the C.A. boatman, is completing a new sharp-bowed Pram for Capt. Nicholson', and later in May of that year that it 'shows a very good turn of speed and is much admired'. The ubiquitous Scow was born.

By November the *Cruising Association Bulletin* was reporting that 'An effort is being made to start a class of sailing Prams, about 11 feet long, with sharp bows. Seven of these little craft are on order from Bran.'

In early 1914 Captain Nicholson founded the Lymington River Sailing Club to organise races for the class. Weekly races were arranged for a season from 15 May to 15 August. The *Cruising Association Bulletin* reported in July, 'The 11ft sailing Pram Class is affording very good sport, thirteen having been built to this class and an average of nine turning up for each weekly race.' However, just a month later in its last issue for almost five years, the bulletin commented, 'Now that sport and pastime have for the moment to go their way and that all are preoccupied in mind or body by sterner business, the association will wish Godspeed to those who have been called to the colours.' Britain had declared war on 4 August and the Club closed down.

After the war Captain Nicholson, who lived at Creek Cottage at the top of Oxey Creek, commissioned Dan Bran to design and build a larger 14ft Pram. It too gained popularity and the earlier 11ft Pram became known as the Lymington Scow to distinguish it from the (14ft) Lymington Pram. The term Pram derives from the Dutch *prame* or *praem* for a ship's dinghy; Scow, from the Dutch *schouw* for a shallow draft ferry boat. (The author rather likes the story, however, that when Dutch trading vessels visited Lymington, their small tenders looked like shoes and influenced not only the future name of the 11ft

Dan Bran's shed, visible to the bottom left of the baths, 1928

Pram, as the Dutch word for shoe is *schoen*, but the design as well!)

Dan lived at Rope Walk Cottage, conveniently next door to the Mayflower Inn, and died in 1950. His shed was considered an eyesore by many and later mysteriously burnt down.

By 1921 the Berthon Boat Company was advertising a Lymington Scow complete for £40 and had produced over 200 by 1948.

By 1930 the Scow type was widespread in the Solent and spread to Chichester Harbour and Burnham-on-Crouch after the Second World War. The design and build

Dan Bran

Berthon Lymington Scow

varied between boat yards, but the variations were minor, such as two thwarts rather than one or an inch or more in length or freeboard.

Dan Bran's creation proved to be so suitable for its purpose that it spread far and wide. He may have received little education, but he knew the local waters and what was required of a small boat to cope with them. He could not have known, however, that over 100 years later, the design would be essentially unchanged and still very popular.

Berthon Lymington Scow General Plan

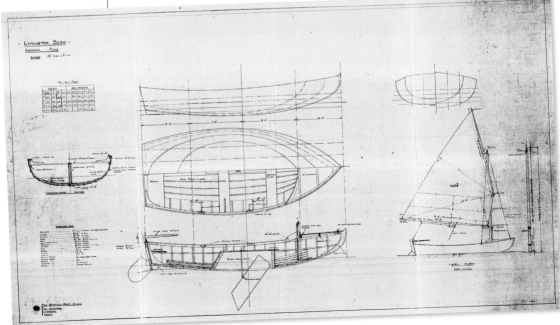

During the Second World War, fibreglass was used to make photo-reconnaissance boxes for aircraft such as the Mosquito by a company which later became Halmatic, one of the pioneers of GRP as a boat-building material. They were sourcing new products after the war when it is said that one of the directors took a mould off a Scow, therefore possibly becoming the first leisure boat in the UK to be constructed in fibreglass. The mould is said to have later been acquired by the Palace Quay Boatyard at Beaulieu, which produced West Solent Scows.

In 1984 Dr Jonathan Rogers started Wednesday Junior Sailing at the Royal Lymington YC, introducing many more local children to sailing. It used a fleet of budget-priced Avon Scows loaned by Club Members, produced in Christchurch by another accomplished Lymington boat builder, John Claridge, using GRP hulls.

John was keen to build a better-quality product and developed a boat based on the Palace Quay Boatyard West Solent Scow, launching it in 1990, the first one being given the sail number 250 to avoid confusion with previous Scows. Junior Sailing, led now by Roger Wilson, wanted to replace the Avon Scows and felt the new boat would be excellent for Junior Sailing, as well as for one-design racing and pottering down rivers and through marshes. Junior Sailing suggested some modifications, including improved buoyancy, and this boat became the Lymington River Scow to distinguish it from the earlier wooden clinker-built Lymington Scow. Lymington sail maker Pete Sanders (whose first commercial sail was for a Lymington Scow) made the sails; uniquely for a Scow it had the option of a jib. It cost just over £3,500 on the water. However, as a gesture of support for Junior Sailing, John offered to sell them to Club Members for £2,350 in part-finished form, as long as the owner made the boat available for use by Wednesday Junior Sailing. Junior Sailing (Ruth Evans in

Lymington River Scow Class Association 'Tell Tale Trophy'. A silver-framed original advertisement by the Berthon Boat Co Ltd for a Lymington Scow, from a 1921 edition of the Yachting Monthly, with the description: 'A Practical Present, This Boat Complete for £40'

Scows in Oxey Lake

particular, but also Roger Wilson, Roly Stafford and others) finished the boats at no charge to the owners, and 15 were kept free of charge on the Club's pontoon. This had the dual effect of not only building a fleet to teach the growing number of children, but also of building a fleet for adults; further boats were ordered from John Claridge.

Lymington River Scows started to appear regularly at Monday evening dinghy racing and in 1994, the then Rear Commodore Sailing, Malcolm McKeag, asked Roly Stafford to start a Club Scow division with the objective of growing the fleet ('An uncharacteristic lapse of good judgement on his part', wrote Roly; 'Perhaps in the same mood, I accepted.'). Roly served as Captain of the Royal Lymington YC Scow Division for three years (alternately being referred to as Captain of Capsize rather than Captain of Scows!), during which time an adventurous cruising ('pottering') in-company programme was developed, and racing grew in popularity.

An extensive programme of pottering, racing and social activities developed and is very popular.

For six months of the year from April to October the division organises weekly potters in company on a Thursday; during October, after racing has finished, these are held twice a week. They can vary from a short sail through the lakes before lunch, to a picnic cruise to destinations such as Hurst Spit, Newtown Creek, Pitts Deep, Colwell Bay or the Yar river. A highlight is 'Threading the Needles'.

At the time of printing the Club has 51 boats registered for racing on a Monday night divided into two fleets: gold and silver.

The division runs four annual special events:

⚓ The Figure of Eight race is a weekend race describing a figure of eight around Oxey and Pylewell Islands.

There are also three series of four short races on Tuesday evenings for:

⚓ The Alexina Trophy, a half-model of a Scow which is displayed in the Clubhouse bar, donated by Simon Williams-Thomas in memory of his wife, a well-loved member of the class.

⚓ The Hinxman Trophy, a silver cup donated by the Hinxman family.

⚓ The Captain's Trophy, a glass plaque donated by Sebastian Chamberlain and made by Jane Pitt-Pitts.

The Christine Sutherland Cup, the 'Victor Ludorum' trophy of the division, is awarded to the sailor who has the lowest aggregate score from the Club's Monday evening racing, the division's four annual one-day events and the LRSCA's National Championship. The division also runs an annual Scow Inter-Club Challenge, initiated by Sebastian Chamberlain.

Other Club Scow events include the annual Lymington Dinghy Regatta, Youth Week, the Potter Dinghy Race and the December Peter Andreae and Penguin Trophies. Youth Week, held the week after Cowes Week, sees some

Overleaf:
LR Scows threading
the needles

A wonderful little boat for exploring the Solent creeks

30 young crews in Scows having a great deal of fun! The Club first ran the Lymington River Scow National Championship for the LRSCA in 2000 and subsequently ran five others (in 2002, 2004, 2007, 2011 and 2015).

Left:
Young sailors racing Scows at the mouth of the River

Below:
Scows starting a race on the Club line

Some of the Members who appear more frequently at the front of the fleet provide race training through talks in the winter and on-the-water sessions in the summer. Sailing is replaced by walks, talks and suppers during the winter.

Other highlights of the social programme are the pre-season Spring Back to Scowing supper, the Annual Dinner after the AGM (normally in November) and the Christmas Cheer supper. Informal suppers are also held during the winter.

The division has some 180 members who own around 120 Lymington River Scows. The Club owns a further 14, 12 of which are for Junior Sailing and two for Members' use.

Conclusion

From its conception before the First World War by an eccentric but consummate Lymington boat builder to its modern incarnation by another talented Lymington boat builder, the Scow has appealed to many sailors over many years. A desire to race the original Lymington Scow inspired the

creation of the first Lymington Sailing Club. Later, the modern Lymington River Scow became the most numerous class of boat in the Western Solent.

The Lymington River Scow is colourful, attractive and well built. It is simple and easy to trail, launch, sail, store and maintain. It is versatile; ideal for teaching, pottering, racing, rowing, motoring with an outboard, single- or double-handed, with the family and the dog! It appeals across ages, experience and competencies, from beginners to experts, juniors to 'masters'. It is one-design, enabling class racing without the need for handicaps. It has well organised associations, an overall class association and separate club sections, which support comprehensive pottering, racing and social programmes for like-minded people.

The Lymington River Scow is 30 years old and, in 2021, the class celebrated its 25th National Championship. As Sebastian Chamberlain once put it, 'The Royal Lymington YC Scow Division is truly one of the great success stories of that wonderful Club.'

As Roly Stafford said, 'The future looks more than promising.' ⚓

Preparing to go racing

A family complete with dog cruising these wonderful little boats at Keyhaven.

13 XOD Class at 100+

Richard Field, Royal Lymington Yacht Club Member, X Class Historian, and Lymington X Class member since 1974, reviews the evolution of the XOD at the Royal Lymington Yacht Club.

The origins of the 'X' One Design Class and the Royal Lymington Yacht Club share a number of similarities.

Both were founded in 1922, struggled at first in the difficult post-First World War years, passed thresholds in 1925 and succeeded through the work of some dynamic and inspiring individuals, some shared between them. It is great fun to see their efforts show up in the *Yachtsman* magazine, published weekly between 1892 and 1939 from a small office in the Strand next to Somerset House and packed full of first-hand reports. What follows is based on these.

Pre-1914, the name of our Club's founder, plain Cyril H. Potter, can be brilliantly found amongst the entries in the news and society columns of the *Yachtsman*, referring to people like Princess Beatrice, Queen Victoria's daughter, and her friend, ex-Empress Eugenie of France, cruising the Solent in their fabulous steam yachts. Around 1908 Potter is already described as a

X173 Heyday, helmed by RLymYC member Gill Clark who is the current Secretary of the 'X' One Design Class Association

XOD's 'goose-winging' in the last century

Royal Yacht Squadron member and a prominent member of the Royal Victoria YC at Ryde, then a major club which ran the Olympic sailing that year. He was their Commodore, I believe. One year there is a super photograph of him in his 61-ton cruising yacht *Nevada*. And he is so young, only just over 30.

The only reports for Lymington before the First World War are lovely, detailed ones of the regattas held each year in the third week of August on a Wednesday, early closing day. They are totally town events, run for 30 years or so by Charles King of Kings of Lymington bookshop, including races for fishing boats and other locals, with the whole town 'en fete' and jollities carrying on up the High Street in the evening.

Posh yachting people joined in, such as the Redwings who came over from Bembridge, and loved it, all races finishing upriver near the Baths. Yarmouth with the Solent YC was the big yachting venue in the Western

Opposite: Richard and Liz Field's XOD Persephone dressed overall for the Club's Centenary Regatta

YACHT RACING AT LYMINGTON

XOD's in the Lymington River. The River is now too busy for XOD starts from the Club line

Solent at this time and their large annual regattas immediately followed the Lymington one.

As regards the future X One Design Class, their beginnings date to the arrival of the six much-anticipated new Royal Motor YC OD club boats (later the X boats) at Netley in June 1911, which is fully and excitedly reported on. All their points and regatta races are included weekly right through to 1914, especially the brilliant ladies' races. There were many changes after the war, and even big yacht clubs struggled and nearly went under.

The Xs first appear in 1920, still known as the RMYC ODs, when the Royal Motor Yacht Club restarted in a cabin on the end of Hythe Pier, with the usual race reports following as before. They appeared for the first time as the X' One Design Class in 1922, the enterprising Royal Motor having taken the fantastic decision to promote the boats as an open class. That year they were listed as XODs at Cowes Week for the first time, although only two raced. The fleets were similarly very small at all the Club and regatta races from 1922–24. There must have been concerns over whether the class would survive.

1921 saw fun news for our Club: the Potters arrived in the Western Solent, father and mother Potter and their two daughters Sheila and Bettine, all racing Solent Seabirds at Yarmouth. How lovely for them to find a place and boats they clearly liked. And Mrs Potter (Ida) won a race in Cowes Week in the Seabird Class that year. They'd soon had a new one built for themselves; they were an old Yarmouth Class of heavy 18ft clinker centre-boarders, safe but nice to sail and race.

Then, in 1922, father Potter decided to have a go at starting a yacht club across the water at Lymington, and what a go he made of it, the whole family being involved and using their private house as the first Clubhouse. We know that the Seabirds were the first class the Club supported, with regular racing from early June to September. At Yarmouth they tended to follow the Season (including Goodwood, Ascot, Wimbledon and Cowes week etc.) and didn't start until July 16.

Neither Lymington nor its Club features in the *Yachtsman* from 1920–23.

Then, magically, in 1924, the first report of the Lymington River Sailing Club appears, a short article about the regatta run by the Club. I missed it at first, because the town was no longer involved. But the beautiful West Solents had arrived; Major and Mrs Potter had one each. A large photograph shows her in her winning number 1 Arrow. The Hon. Mrs Angela Brownlow is also in the fleet, bringing her glamour and style to the class and Club.

In 1925 a much bigger regatta report is published, now under the Club's name, with three XODs competing, two down from Hythe, their very first showing here.

Finally in 1926 a full report appears of the Club's AGM in April, when it was reconstituted as the Lymington Yacht Club and Major Cyril Potter was elected Commodore for life in recognition of all he'd done: fantastic to see. And from then on regular race reports and the Club's activities feature regularly in the *Yachtsman*.

The XOD Class also made a breakthrough in 1925 when the Parkstone Sailing Club adopted the class, formed its own division and had boats built in Poole. They came to Cowes that year and stayed on for a brilliant team race at Hythe against the Royal Motor. A double page spread of the latter appeared in the magazine.

In December 1926, Tipperary-born Admiral Sir Sackville Hamilton Carden started the Lymington X division from our Club, and the first Berthon-built boats sailed here in 1927. Despite his high status and bearing an awful cross for Gallipoli, he was personable and attracted friends and followers. In 1928 the Earl of Essex joined our Club and the Lymington X

15th July 2018 – Lymington XOD week – arriving at the windward mark. The Paton's XL in the lead

Class, with him in a Berthon boat.

The Xs rested when Carden died suddenly in early 1930 but started up again with a bang in 1946.

Amidst all the racing ever since for points and cups, two things come to mind:

One is Joan Braithwaite introducing after-race teas in 1980. Before that, we tailenders queued at the bar for a beer when it opened, the front of fleet

75 Delight and *93* Margaret racing in the Solent in the last century. Sadly Margaret was destroyed by fire whilst being maintained at Ampress in 1999

gods having long gone. We got to know people this way. A vital X-Class institution from Poole to Itchenor, at some places (like Yarmouth) the sailors' wives still provide the cakes, cream teas being served if they are very lucky.

The other is the Invitation Race run in Xs from the 1960s for 30 years or so, with guests sailing our boats. It was held in late September, with a superbly liquid lunch in the Club afterwards. The following were invited:

- ⚓ The Mayor and Town Council.
- ⚓ Hampshire Cricket Club.
- ⚓ The Ferry skippers, often two, plus a crew member. We got to know them and one became an Honorary Member.
- ⚓ The Customs: a lady in a tight skirt turned up once; we had to find her a life jacket.
- ⚓ The Police, fearless and great fun.
- ⚓ The Marina.
- ⚓ Cross Channel ferry skippers once, a hoot.
- ⚓ The Harbour Master.
- ⚓ The fishermen; we were over the moon when one came regularly.
- ⚓ Lymington Town SC Commodore.
- ⚓ Keyhaven YC Commodore.
- ⚓ And more.

Usually, we had between 10 and 12 boats out; once we had to reef, and they sailed superbly. The Commodore and his wife came to lunch and he welcomed the guests. It was a lovely thing for us to be able to do for the Club and the neighbourhood. It was the brainchild of Terence Gossage, such a super chap.

And now in the Xs we are so lucky to have 30 plus moorings all in a row, magically arranged for us by Derf Paton, with smart boats to go on them. Last year one was X18 *Nefertiti*, built at Berthon in 1927 for the Perkins family, founder Members, still racing fast at the front of the fleet, getting a gun at Cowes.

I am most grateful for being allowed to write these brief reflections. ⚓

14 Wednesday Junior Sailing – Started in 1984 and Still Going Strong.

The Royal Lymington Yacht Club is immensely proud of its pioneering Junior Sailing project, which is designed to get local youngsters afloat and having fun, regardless of how much money they have and which school they attend. Ruth Evans, a stalwart of Wednesday Junior Sailing, wrote this introduction in 1999. It is still accurate today. Current Rear Commodore Sailing Jenny Wilson provides a brief history of the evolution of WJS

HRH The Princess Royal talking with Ali Husband, chief of WJS, and her team at the 35th Anniversary in 2019

Wednesday Junior Sailing (WJS) is a scheme run by the Royal Lymington Yacht Club for any child between the ages of eight and eighteen who, with the consent of their parents, likes to turn up on Wednesday afternoons between April and September from 2pm to 6pm to experience the delights of sailing. No charge is made for tuition, but each child is charged £1 to cover the cost of a drink and a doughnut.

Preparing for Wednesday Junior Sailing

The scheme was started in 1984 by Dr Jonathan Rogers and Dr Tom McEwen to give local children, for whom there were no other opportunities, a chance to get involved in sailing. To get the scheme going, he built the first four Avon Scows, one for himself and one each for three of his friends. These were quickly followed by other Club Members offering to lend their Scows; soon there was a fleet of 10 or 11 boats. Support was also forthcoming from Members with motorboats, who offered their services as rescue boats. Local firms generously donated buoyancy aids and sponsored Optimist dinghies. The RYA also helped with encouragement and advice. Space was then needed for all the boats so Jonathan, a handful of Club Members and the Club boatman built a floating pontoon in front of the Clubhouse. Today (1999) the Club has the loan of 17 Scows and owns 24 Oppies.

WJS has always been run by volunteers, not all of whom are Members of RLymYC. In the early days most had sailed all their lives, but none had recognised qualifications. With the increasing number of children and the need for formal tuition, the RYA's teaching syllabus was adopted and the helpers were encouraged to take courses to qualify as RYA dinghy instructors or safety-boat drivers. Many have now qualified as senior instructors and the Club is recognised as an RYA teaching establishment. In 1995 WJS was acclaimed nationally and, at a presentation at the RYA Nautical Awards at the Café Royal, received the inaugural Yacht Club Community Award.

The initial take up was about 30 children, and Scows and a number of Optimists were used. When Jonathan Rogers retired from running the Wednesday sessions in 1993, Roger Wilson took over as Head of WJS and Head of the RYA teaching establishment. This was around the time of the Lyme Bay canoeing accident, after which the regulations for running such activities were tightened up. The RYA and the Adventure Activities Licencing Authority (AALA) required formal risk assessments and safety policies and began annual inspections. New boats were required with better buoyancy.

Discussions between local boatbuilder John Claridge and Roger Wilson resulted in a re-designed Scow with built-in buoyancy tanks: the Lymington River Scow was born. Club Members were able to purchase the hulls for a special price, the fitting out and maintenance being done by Ruth Evans and Roger Wilson. The agreement was that the Scows were lent to the children on Wednesday afternoons and for Junior Regatta week, in return for free berthing on the Club pontoon and owner use at any other time. Thirteen Members signed up for the deal and over the winter the boats were built and fitted out ready for the next season. Local businesses also continued to sponsor a number of Optimist dinghies. The fleet at this time numbered around 35 dinghies.

With this new fleet of boats, WJS went from strength to strength and by 1998, the end of season report on attendance shows that 363 children had taken part, with an average of 108 each week. It was calculated that there had been 2,042 child sessions during the season, assisted by 80 volunteers and 10 older juniors. There was no difficulty in attracting children and it was not unusual for 150 to turn up on a nice summer's day.

However, the report also mentions that new volunteers were needed. The apparently effortless way in which WJS runs is due to the tremendous amount of work put in by volunteers, and recruiting and training new volunteers is an essential part of keeping it running, not to mention the ongoing fund-raising required to keep the boats in good order.

The shore volunteers who ran the WJS office and those who taught the children to rig boats, tie knots, learn theory and how to row in the Club tenders, were absolutely invaluable.

The Junior Regatta in August each year was, for many junior sailors taking part in WJS, their first opportunity to take part in some formal racing. The Optimist Fleet, using the Club Oppies and managed by Stuart Jardine for many years, saw 20 or so children each year getting to grips with racing in Oxey Lake, encouraged over a megaphone by Stuart's vast enthusiasm.

The LR Scow Fleet often numbered 30 boats, divided into two or three starts; numbering about 90 young sailors, it tended to be noisy and exuberant.

Ali Husband briefs the volunteers before WJS– and it takes a lot of volunteers ashore and afloat to make it work!

The older WJS sailors were encouraged to take out some of the younger and less experienced children, and a great deal of fun was had by all. At the start of the week many had to be rescued from lee shores and coached upwind, but by the end, most of the children had improved hugely, although the race officer had probably lost his or her voice!

The Solent Fleet comprised many sailors who had started at WJS and gone on to sail high performance boats, often taking part in national and international events. Regatta week was an opportunity to swap boats with friends, try out new exciting boats and socialise most evenings at the many barbecue venues offered by helpful Club Members.

Expedition Day was for many children the high point of the week, though for the volunteers running it, a potential nightmare! The whole regatta fleet decamped to Newtown or more latterly Sowley, involving a pursuit race to get there, a picnic on the beach and then a race home. The dinghies were all tied in strings to the back of the motherships, whose owners had generously offered their craft as comfort for the terrified and had anchored off the beach. It was a fine sight to see all the boats with their strings of dinghies bobbing gently off the shore. The turn of the tide in the middle of the day caused a few entanglements and a few capsizes, but were sorted out by a small team of dedicated safety boats. By the return race, the sea breeze had generally set in and a number of the social sailors decided that a trip home on the mothership was far more desirable than sailing home. The stalwarts were delivered back into their boats and set off into a building sea breeze for the race home. It has been fascinating over the years to hear from now-adult former WJ Sailors who remember the race home as one of the defining memories of their young lives.

In 2000, Roger Wilson stood down from the role of Head of WJS, although he continued to run the RYA Training Centre and participate regularly. His wife Jenny, who had assisted at WJS since he took over and had trained first as a DI and then as a SI, took over the day-to-day running of WJS. The Wednesday sessions continued as before with the addition of a Lymington Pram, built by John Claridge, to the fleet. Bigger and more solid than a Scow, this was an excellent boat for taking out some of the children

with disabilities, who attended regularly and enjoyed short excursions on the water.

We were also delighted to be allowed to use some of the Club rowing dinghies each week and gradually a team of rowing instructors was built up with a very keen following; a number of the children preferring rowing to sailing.

At this time, we were lucky to have some older teenagers staying on to help teach the newcomers. A system of junior instructor training was introduced; willing helpers were rewarded by being trained as assistant instructors with a view to becoming dinghy instructors once they turned 16.

Although there was a card system whereby each child was issued with a coloured test card encased in plastic and worn round the neck, ticking off the tasks was not essential, and if the children just wanted to enjoy being on the water, there was no compulsion to get anything signed off. The atmosphere was lovely, like a sailing youth club with older children taking out younger ones and sometimes just pottering about in boats chatting to friends.

Sharks and pirates – sometimes a problem for mariners

In 2002 we were excited to hear from Club Secretary Ian Gawn that Dirk Kalis from Lymington Yacht Haven had offered to sponsor WJS for 10 years. It was wonderful to know that the continuation of the project was assured and that boats and equipment could be updated. One of the conditions of the agreement was that RIB-driving training should be brought in for the children, generating much excitement. It also meant that the Scow fleet could be updated and some of the original Scows that had been sold or removed from the pontoon could gradually be replaced.

The Haven Scows with their black hulls and brightly coloured sails appeared: one new scow each year for the next few years, bearing names such as *Haven Sent, Good Havens* and *Just Havenly*. A new, large RIB,

WJS showing a variety of craft

Golden Haven, joined the safety boat ranks and was invaluable supporting Wednesday afternoons, Regatta Week and the growing number of training sessions run at the weekends for the increasing junior fleets.

At the prize-giving that year, congratulations were also given for the great achievement of 10-year-old Thomas Morgan, another Wednesday Junior Sailor, who competed in the final of the Honda/RYA Youth RIB Challenge at the Southampton Boat Show and won first place in the Junior Class. The prize: a brand-new RIB for the Royal Lymington Yacht Club!

By 2008, volunteers to run WJS, especially senior instructors, were becoming rather thin on the ground and during busy times such as Cowes Week, some of the sessions had to be cancelled. No one was keen to take

Clockwise from top:
When hiking out goes wrong...

Teamwork

Foredeck grappling with the
kite; Helm giving instructions...
was it ever thus

over the role of Head of WJS and there was also an ongoing problem with boat maintenance, as a number of the older helpers were stepping down. The decision was made to advertise for a senior instructor who could work at

"Trouble? What trouble?" The legendary (and much missed) Roly Stafford (first Club Captain of Scows) provides advice

the Club one day a week, performing maintenance and helping to run sessions with a view to being the SI in charge if one of the regular volunteers was unable to do the job. Enter Kristy Powell, a bright, cheery, enthusiastic SI, who brought a breath of fresh air to the proceedings. The children loved her and her enthusiasm was infectious. Knowing that she would be there every week brought a much-needed respite for the SI team.

2009 saw the 25th Anniversary of the founding of WJS and a big party was planned. Our Patron HRH The Princess Royal, to our delight, accepted an invitation to join the proceedings. She duly arrived and after talking to the volunteers in the office and on the pontoons, enjoyed meeting many of the children and went afloat in *Golden Haven* to watch the children sail and chat to them on the water. One of the challenges for them was to come alongside the RIB to have a chat with her without knocking anyone out! It was slightly nerve-wracking as the potential for disaster was high, but all went well and the children were proud to show off their sailing achievements. The

Previous page: HRH the Princess Royal names a new Scow at the WJS 35th Anniversary in 2019. The crowd of volunteers and young sailors gives an idea of how many volunteers and young sailors attend WJS every Wednesday afternoon during the season.

rowers demonstrated their rowing and sculling skills, and her visit was rounded off with some speeches and the cutting of a lovely anniversary cake made by chef Peter Lowe. After her departure the children enjoyed sampling the cake and playing games.

At the end of 2009 both Roger and Jenny Wilson felt that it was time to step down after 16 years of running WJS. David Simpson agreed to take over the role of Head of the Training Establishment and Edward Harrison-Jeive took over the role of Head of WJS.

The project was in a good place financially thanks to the Yacht Haven, and Kristy Powell was able to oversee the sessions on the day and help with maintenance and training. The next chapter was set in motion.

The next four years saw a few changes, with RS Teras being introduced for the benefit of the better sailors, but all continued to run smoothly. Edward stepped down as Head of WJS at the end of 2013 and Ali Husband took up the reins for the 2014 season, the 30th anniversary of the project. ⚓

WEDNESDAY JUNIOR SAILING ACHIEVEMENTS

1999	Nick Thompson	European Champion	Optimist
2000	Jemima Marshall	World Team	420
2000	Dominic Hutton	World Team	Laser Radial
2000	Luke Cross	World Team	Laser Radial
2001	Oren Richards	World Team	Cadet
2003	Robbie Claridge	World Team	Optimist
2003	Greg Carey	National Champion	Optimist
2005	Poppy Husband	World Team	420
2006	Poppy Husband	World Team	420
2007	Poppy Husband	World Team	420
2007	Ben Paton	World Champion	Laser Radial
2007	Jasmine Husband	Junior Women's European Champion	420
2008	Nick Rogers	Olympic Silver	470

2008	Pippa Wilson	Olympic Gold	Yngling
2010	Greg Carey	National Champion	Laser Standard
2010	Nick Thompson	World's Silver/Ranked 2nd in the world	Laser
2010	Andrew Smith	National Champion	Cadet
2011	Robbie Claridge	National Champion	Scow
2011	Ben Paton	World's Bronze	International Moth
2012	Jess Eales	Ladies National Champion	RS Feva
2012	Richard Mason	World Championship Silver	470
2012	Richard Mason	Artemis Sailing Academy single handed ocean sailing	
2012	Sophie Weguelin	European Women's Champion	470
2012	Tom Britz	Youth National Champion	SL16
2012	Tom Britz	World Champion	SL16
2012	Harry Fitzsimmons	World Team	Cadet
2012	Robbie Claridge	National Champion	Scow
2013	Tom Britz	Youth National Champion	Spitfire
2013	Hattie Rogers	Girls National Champion	Optimist
2013	Hattie Rogers	Irish National Champion	Optimist
2013	Hattie Rogers	First Girl – Bermuda Gold Cup	Optimist
2013	Millie Boyle	Girls Nationals Silver	Optimist
2014	Jess Eales	Represented country at ISAF Youth Worlds	Spitfire
2014	James Eady	RYA Honda Southern Region Powerboat Champion	
2014	Tom Rogers	RYA Champion of Clubs RIB Race Gold	
2018	Harry West	RS Tera Worlds Third	RS Tera Sport
2019	Vita Heathcote	Worlds First Women's Fleet	420
2019	Milly Boyle	Worlds First Women's Fleet	420
2019	Tim Hire	UK Youth Championships First	RS Aero
2019	Abby Hire	Worlds Third Overall & First Girl	RS Feva
2021	Vita Heathcote	European Championships Bronze	470
2022	Hattie Rogers	Sail GP Inspire Racing Female Champion	WASZP

Clockwise from far left:

Optimist sailing can be a wet experience

David Weller teaching a mixed age-group class sailing theory

Ice cream time

Left:
Aerial view of WJS
35th Anniversary
celebrations, also
showing the area
cordoned off due
to erosion of the
sea wall

Overleaf:
Rowing practice in
the club tenders

*Previous page
HRH The Princess
Royal names "Royal
Coral" at the 35th
Anniversary of WJS*

*Right:
Swimming and
having fun – part of
confidence building
on (and in) the water*

*Below:
Young sailors can
start sailing as
passengers, then
crew, and then
helming*

15 Royal Lymington Olympians

The notice board pictured on the right shows those Members who have represented Great Britain at the Olympics and those who have won Olympic medals.

Ado Jardine

'In 1959 and 60, I was based in Germany in the Army and with very few FDs in the UK and big fleets in Europe I did the European circuit; plus the Olympic selectors set all seven series in Europe, from which they would make their selection!! That was how my results in these seven series were recorded under "miscellaneous" in the 1960 bulletin. However, you can see from the sailing detail that I was one of the reserves. One of the selectors selected himself without doing any of the seven series, saying I was young enough to have a go again in the future and, at 65, it was his last chance!!!! I wrote an unbelievably rude letter to the RYA and selectors; he finished up seventh. So having finished second in the World Championship and a favourite for a medal that time, it all came to nothing...

Talking about selection nonsenses, the Finn Class selection was also stupid; initially for the Sydney games

Past Commodore and current
Trustee Geoff Holmes with
Nick Rogers, Sir Ben Ainslie
and Pippa Wilson

they set a minimum wind speed because it was going to be windy, but forgot what they had said so sent Richard Creagh-Osborne to Sydney and our heavyweight, Vernon Stratton, to Naples and its light winds!!!'

Pippa Wilson (Kenton-Page) MBE

'Being part of the sailing community at the Royal Lymington Yacht Club has been a huge honour for me and probably the single most significant part of my young life. The opportunity to train and race at such a high level from such a young age and be surrounded by the most committed volunteers and the highest standards of sailing is something that I will be forever grateful for and which led me on my path to Olympic Gold. Sailing and the community it offers will now always be a huge part of my life and something that I love to share with my own family. I feel very lucky to have been part of such a special club in such a beautiful part of the world, and The Royal Lymington Yacht Club for me will always feel like home.'

Ben Ainslie CBE

'It's wonderful to see so many friendly faces. It's down to this Club and others around the country which give us such great support for the sport. It's important we build on this and give all these youngsters a chance to enjoy the same thing.' ⚓

16 MacNamara's Bowl –
The Start of it All...

Rosemary Johnson (nee Taylor), stalwart of many MacNamara Bowl campaigns, writes about the history of this famous event, ably assisted by Titch Blachford – multiple Bowl winner.

Sometime in 1978, Brian MacNamara was in Cherbourg and chanced upon a French yacht raced and crewed entirely by women. They regaled him with their stories and adventures. In all probability, they had been competing in an all-female series of races along the south Brittany coast that summer. The event was not a one-off and had been going for some time, well organised and (more importantly) sponsored, as the French do so well. Brian told them they must come over to Lymington and challenge our ladies. He realised we had no equivalent event on this side of the Channel so on return he promoted the idea with the enthusiastic support of the likes of Eileen Caulcutt. Brian provided the trophy, a silver bowl won in India by his father at a polo event. The Club insisted it carried his name and so the event was born.

From its foundation in 1922, women have been busy in the RLymYC. The first Rear Commodore was The Hon. Mrs Cecil Brownlow, the only female Commodore ever elected before or since. Other female Members like Helen Tew became famous when, aged 89, she fulfilled her lifetime ambition of sailing the Atlantic.

In the 1950s a wind of change blew across the UK. Women's place in society had changed during the Second World War: they had taken the place of men in the factories and the fields. They also served in the armed forces, as WRACs, WAAFs and WRENs. They made munitions and parachutes and cared for the wounded in Red Cross hospitals. Things had changed. By the 1960s and 1970s, a feminist movement was in full swing.

Perhaps this was what influenced Rosemary Johnson and Fiona Rogers, Lymington housewives and mothers, to get an all-girl racing crew together. Husbands, sailing friends and male Members of the Club were surprisingly encouraging and gave advice and useful training. The girls actually won in *Blue Heron* in 1979. Various women friends were invited to join – among them Val Chorley, Jane Adley, Romy Halliwell, Helen Johnson, Sally Potter, Sally Sergeaunt, Rachel Kalis, Cam Otten, Judy Ruffell and, later, Sue Hawkes, Ros Bond, Christine Robinson and many others.

Blue Heron crew, from the left: Rosemary Johnson, Rachel Kalis, Jane Ardley, Fiona Rogers and Val Chorley in 1978

These young women soon became confident enough to take out their own boats in competition. Howard Lewis, the wonderful Club Secretary at that time, could often be seen anchored in the Solent, covertly checking that the all-women crews were safe. Soon Contessas *Hullabaloo*, *Greenshank*, *Kingdom Come*, *Assent* and *Contiguity* were also to be seen out on the water. They broke the mould and competed regularly in the RLymYC Wednesday afternoon keel boat races, which *Blue Heron* won in 1979.

Fiona and Rosemary would often go back to the Club after putting the boat to bed to enjoy a refreshing drink in the bar. Brian MacNamara, a keen Captain of Cruising, was often to be found there. He used to tease Fiona and Rosemary, saying that on a recent sailing trip to France he had come across an all-female crew who were so much more adept than they were – and prettier too!

Eventually they returned his banter, saying that if these French girls were so good, why shouldn't they be invited over here for a competitive race. Brian readily agreed – he had been plotting this all the time, with a twinkle in his Irish eye! He offered a magnificent trophy for the winning boat. So the MacNamara Bowl Regatta was conceived. This was to be, as far as it's known, the first international all-female competition for racing yachts anywhere in the world.

Eileen Caulcutt, Rear Commodore Sailing, was enthusiastic and immensely helpful in setting up the Regatta, even taking part in her own boat. Many owners of Contessa 32s kindly lent their boats to women Members who wished to compete. The number of all-female boats multiplied throughout the Club and even spread to neighbouring yacht clubs. The French accepted the challenge and there were also entries from the Netherlands and Rhode Island. The Club rallied round with safety boats, race officers and spectator boats: there was real excitement on the water.

In 1978 the first MacNamara Bowl Regatta took place. There were to be two days of three races over the weekend, with a celebration dinner on the Saturday evening and prize giving for competitors after the race on Sunday. There were offers of overnight accommodation for visiting crews. Yacht Haven owner Dirk Kalis offered free berthing for those taking part. Seven

Above:
Rosemary Johnson with the MacNamara Bowl
in 1978.

Right:
Thank heavens that's over!

boats lined up for the start. There were five entries from the home club, one from Ireland and of course the French team, who were the favourites. The racing was close, well sailed and hard fought.

Although each of the competing boats had finished in the first three of at least one race, the three winning boats were *Blue Heron*, *Greenshank* and the Irish *Kingdom Come*. Satisfyingly, the French team was defeated and the first MacNamara Bowl trophy went to the home club's Rosemary Johnson and her young pioneers in *Blue Heron*.

The Mac's Bowl was held annually thereafter, with increasing numbers of foreign girls coming over to compete. The competition, naturally, became keener over the years, with improved standards of sailing and boat handling. Many women had been crewing regularly in Admiral's Cup championships. Titch Blachford, outright winner of Mac's Bowl in 1984, was already showing herself to be outstanding and helmed the women's team in the Tour de France à la Voile. Debbie Gorrod, winner in 1985, went on to compete in the Women's World Sailing Championship later that year.

What had started in Lymington as a small ripple had grown into a full worldwide wave.

The rising popularity of Mac's Bowl meant that by 1983 it had become hard to find enough Contessa 32s for the crews wishing to take part. The Steering Committee decided to change to the lighter and more numerous J24s. Sponsored that year for the first time by Esso Petroleum, the Js were a popular choice among the 10 female crews who assembled to compete for the silver rose bowl. Esso enthusiastically produced T-shirts for all competitors, lavish entertainment and even catering for the crews and spectators. Keen racing was evidenced by the increasing expertise of the crews. A distinctive feature of Mac's Bowl was the general good humour of

The MacNamara Bowl makes the front page of Newsline, the company magazine of sponsor Esso in August 1984

the crews and spectators. There were very few protests, although a committee boat was always there to ensure fair play.

Esso provided a popular, well-stocked spectator boat where, it was reputed, betting on the winners was rife and binoculars were in constant use to watch the many competing ladies. The local press made much of one bikini-clad crew member seen hoisting a sail with a cigarette drooping from her mouth! Hospitality to the visiting crews was generous and greatly appreciated. One year, the Dutch girls, amidst the euphoria of the prize giving, had passed round their offerings of delicious cheese, smoked eels and gin. They went down very well.

The J24 Association gave their support and many local owners loaned their boats. RLymYC ladies visited France, the Netherlands and Rhode Island, where other clubs were following the example of the Mac's Bowl for all-women crews. Dutch Visitors, Hanna Zuiderbaan-Schoen and Anneke van Loewen in particular, came almost every year to compete. Even Princess Anne, the Club's patron, attended the Regatta in 1991, sailing in a stiff breeze with Titch Blachford on her winning boat *Smokey Four*. Sally Potter, Rear Commodore Sailing, accompanied the Princess and remembers reminding Her Royal Highness as they went into a very windy gybe at the bottom mark, to 'Mind Your Backside Ma'am!'

Titch was to go on and win many more Mac's Bowls until 1995 which was the last recorded Regatta. By then there was no need for an all-female regatta. Women had proved a point and been recognised as proficient and capable sailors. Sponsors were no longer interested in funding what had become commonplace. Competitor numbers had dwindled. In a word, the Mac's Bowl Regatta had become a victim of its own success. But the RLymYC can be proud of the fact that it was the first to encourage women to take an equal role in keel boat racing, in a movement that became worldwide.

Some of the Mac's Bowl pioneers have told me what it had meant to them 40 plus years later:

'The one thing Mac's Bowl did for me was to prove to myself that I could overcome my fear and get around a course without sinking!'
Cam Otten

'I thought it was great fun –
I learnt a lot and made a
lot of lasting friends.'
Val Chorley

'It was exciting, challenging, and gave me a sense of achievement.'
Judy (Elliot) Ruffel:

'Sailing competently as a woman generated for me a fulfilling, competitive spirit which totally embraces all the senses.'
Sally Kalis (Potter)

LIST OF WINNERS OF MACNAMARA BOWL

YEAR	WINNER	BOAT	CLASS	COMMENT
1978	Rosemary Johnson	Blue Heron	Contessa 32	7 boats from UK, Ireland, France
1979	Angela Woods Jane Pitt Pitts	Assent	Contessa 32	13 boats from UK and overseas
1980	Lynne Brown Holly Maledy (Canada)	Blanco	Contessa 32	18 boats from UK, Canada, Netherlands
1981	Trish Ford	Roulette	Contessa 32	12 boats from UK, Ireland
1982	Jessica Nunn	Cantilena	Contessa 32	10 boats from UK, Norway etc
1983	Eileen Caulcutt Trish Ford	Chico Xixia	Contessa 32	7 boats from UK, Netherlands, Ireland

YEAR	WINNER	BOAT	CLASS	COMMENT
1984	Titch Blachford	*Hedgehog*	J24	Change to J24
				10 Boats from UK, Netherlands, Ireland.
				First sponsorship by Esso
1985	Debbie Gorrod	*Tiger*	J24	UK, Netherlands, Ireland
1986	Titch Blachford	*Hedgehog*	J24	20 boats
				UK and others
1987				
1988	Titch Blachford	*Hedgehog*	J24	20 boats
1989	Titch Blachford	*Joint Venture*	J24	First Swiss boat
1990	Titch Blachford	*J24 Jooler*	J24	
	Cathy Ash-Vie	*Nazka*		
	Channel Handicap			
1991	Titch Blachford	*Smokey Four*	J24	Won Caulcutt Cup for overall both fleets
	Carol Strickland			
1992	Titch Blachford	*Smokey Four*	J24	
	Carol Strickland			
	Channel Handicap			
1993	Cordelia Eglin	*Bijoux*	Caulcutt Cup	Last sponsorship from Esso. Sole international
	Sue Hawkes J24		Mac's Bowl	from Croatia.
	Channel Handicap			
1994	Inge Featherstone	*French Beret*		
	Channel Handicap			
1995	Inga Featherstone	*French Beret*		
	Channel Handicap			

17 Thursday Evening Keelboats

Rear Commodore Sailing Jenny Wilson and past Rear Commodore House Roger Wilson explain the origins and history of our Thursday evening racing.

Thursday Night Racing, now called Thursday Evening Keelboats, started in the late 1980s with the encouragement of Peter Bruce. By 1989 it had around 115 competitors entered for the series and now has up to 130 entrants each year with an average of 70-80 boats starting each week at peak season and over 100 starting on a number of occasions!

The core of its success seems to be starting near the river mouth no earlier than 6pm and getting the competitors back to the bar by 8:30pm.

Initially there were several IRC handicap and Club Handicap Classes as well as various one-design classes, including Etchells, RS Elites, J/80s, Folkboats and XODs. To begin with Tony

One of 80+ yachts racing on Thursday evenings in multiple classes

Blachford set the Club handicaps, but when he stepped down as PRO, we changed to an RYA Sailwave programme that changed the handicaps for each race, but started with our own base numbers, which could be a bit

The race teams have to
set courses for yachts
with different sail plans
and different speeds

subjective. We are now using the RYA NHC base numbers for the first time this year (2022), which are more objective.

The Classes have now stabilised on 2 IRC classes, 3 Club Handicap classes, J/80s and Nordic Folkboats, on rolling starts at four-minute intervals, with all communications done by VHF and flags only used to signal recalls and postponements.

For many years the racing started and finished at the platform but this did cause problems with the ferries and gave few good shorten course options. For the last three years we have used a Committee Boat for most starts, initially because the area around the platform has become much shallower and the depth of many of the yachts has increased, with some drawing as much as 2.4m. We found that most weeks we could either not start from the platform or not finish on the platform.

Left:
Nordic Folkboats
racing, June 2018:
Paloma, Lady Linda
and Nordic Bear

Overleaf:
Glorious conditions
for Thursday
Evening Keelboat
racing

With lots of boats on the water keeping a good look out is essential

The use of a Committee Boat enables the starts to be well away from the river mouth and this has dramatically reduced the number of incidents with the ferries and increased our ability to shorten races, especially when the wind dies.

We rely on a large number of volunteers; for the race teams on the Committee Boat, for mark-laying, managing finishes and very importantly, for ferrying the crews to and from their boats. Without these volunteers it would not be possible to run such successful racing, and we are very grateful for their input.

Tony Blachford was the PRO and Handicap Officer for many years, and the Club owes him a great debt of gratitude for making the event so successful. After him Alastair Wilson, Jenny Wilson and Roger Wilson have each taken turns as PRO, but continued with Tony's policies and the racing has continued to be popular with often ~80 yachts on the start line.

18 The RLymYC and the Admiral's Cup (AC)

Peter Bruce, navigator of British AC team yachts Moonshine (1977), Eclipse (1979), Yeoman XXIII (1981) and Indulgence (1983) and British AC team manager (1985), tells the story of our Club's long involvement with what was thought to be the world championship of offshore racing.

The Royal Lymington Yacht Club, henceforth RLymYC, had a strong association with the Admiral's Cup – not to be confused with the America's Cup which was match-racing between just two vessels.

The renowned trophy was the de facto grand prix of world ocean racing from 1957 until 1993, and the most important sporting event of all for a large number of international yacht-racing people. Indeed, the Admiral's Cup completely took over a number of people's lives. The courses involved thee Solent races, (including the Britannia and New York Yacht Club races), the RORC Channel and the Fastnet race. Usually only the very wealthy could afford to mount a challenge. Even gold-winning Olympic sailors like Paul Elvstrom and Rodney Pattison found that some of the tactics they had used successfully to win their medals were not always good enough for the Admiral's Cup.

In the 70s and 80s, ocean racing was probably rated as one of the most important activities that Club Members undertook, and this period has been described as the golden age of yacht racing. In the earlier days of the Admiral's Cup, two RLymYC Club yacht owners were outstanding. The first was Rendall Clark, who kept his racing yachts, all called *Quiver*, on a lower mooring in the Lymington River. The second, boatbuilder Jeremy Rogers, also achieved extraordinary success with *Moonshine*, which he co-owned with Bill Green, and then had the even more successful *Eclipse*. The other notable and prominent RLymYC contribution at that time was by Doug Baverstock, our erstwhile Club boatman, who helped lay the marks in the western Solent for the British team trials and the event itself. For this and other altruistic deeds Doug was awarded the BEM.

The first ever AC event in 1957, which the British narrowly won, only involved the UK and USA but the second, in 1959, included the Dutch. In their team was *Zwerver*, a big powerful Olin Stephens design owned by the Van der Vorm family who have lived close by at Sowley since 1985. Keen observers of the Solent scene will have noticed the *Zwerver* racing mark just west of the Sowley boom which commemorates this fine yacht. She was the top overall individual AC yacht as well as overall winner in the gale-torn 1961 Fastnet race. Whilst the shoal-drafted yawl *Rapparee*, which I was crewing aboard, was still labouring to windward towards The Rock, I remember the magnificent sight of *Zwerver* H1038 flying downwind under strained spinnaker. I wasn't surprised to hear she had won. Otto Van der Vorm, her skipper and owner, was a Member of the Club until he died in 2011.

Quiver III, owned by Rendall Clarke, was the second-best AC yacht individual boat in 1961 behind *Zwerver* but, in spite of this, the Americans were too strong that year and Britain had to be content with being the second best of the five nations that took part. But in 1965 all came good for *Quiver IV*. She

Quiver IV the year after she won the Admiral's Cup as well as being top individual boat. Here she seems to be in a bit of a broach just off the Squadron!

was not only the top boat in the winning British team but also top individual boat. Mike Hobson, Donald Tew, James McGill and Adam Rendal from the Club all sailed in the *Quivers*, plus Richard Bagnall in *Quiver V* only. That year eight nations took part, and the rest of the planet was fast waking up to the fact that the Admiral's Cup was a well-run, major racing-yacht world championship which deserved close attention. Ren Clarke and the many other RLymYC Members on board had much to celebrate, including his key crewman Geoff Wardle, who got to know Ren when they were both imprisoned in Colditz Castle during the Second World War.

British dominance of the AC continued in the 70s with the number of participating nations growing to 19. The eventual UK total of eight team victories out of the 18 times that the Admiral's Cup was held were partly helped by Ted Heath's famous *Morning Cloud*, though actually it was Robin Aisher's yachts, all named *Yeoman*, that contributed most of all to British success and, after that, Arthur Slater's *Prospect of Whitby* and Graham Walker's campaigns. Like Robin Aisher, Graham's initial enthusiasm for winning the Cup turned from a campaign into a crusade. The British had the advantage that all the seriously competitive British yachts were based in the Solent where the great Solent Points Championship was held, often with RORC offshore races in between. This gave the British contenders a permanently established hot fleet in which to hone their skills.

Famous Club Members the Bagnall twins were both involved in the 1973 AC. Richard was helmsman of *Chandanna* in the trials for the British team, while Harvey sailed aboard the Dutch boat *Nymphaea* in the actual event. In 1979 Harvey steered *Inishanier* – a sister ship to *Eclipse* – for the Irish team, until injured in a windy inshore race, while Richard helmed the Ed Dubois Hong Kong team boat *Vanguard* in the AC with Club Member Simon Van der Byl as navigator; this was the year of the big Fastnet storm, and they were pleased to have finished. Richard went on to crew in the Danish Admiral's Cupper *Andelsbanken* in 1991.

Jeremy Rogers and Bill Green, though not very wealthy, built *Moonshine* for the AC in 1977 and most of the crew, such as Jonathan Bradbeer, David Alan-Williams, Phil Crebbin and myself, were Club Members. However, to begin with, the boat was not given much credibility, as a first timer in the trials. It was the longstanding contestant Chris Dunning's new *Marionette* that was initially cleaning up that year, but the Lymington boat was selected for the team and came on the boil just at the right time to be the top boat in the winning team, which included *Marionette* and *Yeoman XX*. *Moonshine* was second overall in the Fastnet and second overall in the Admiral's Cup individual standings. Club Member Adrian Jardine was aboard *Yeoman XX*.

Jeremy boldly went for another AC boat in 1979 and was selected for the team, along with *Morning Cloud* and Ernest Juer's *Blizzard*. The modest – by Admiral's Cup standards – 39ft *Eclipse* emerged as the top individual AC boat overall, having triumphed over the storm, but it was not a happy year for her much vaunted team mates who trailed far behind on points.

In 1983 I was added to the navigation team of *Yeoman 23*, the yacht which, along with *Victory* and *Dragon*, formed what would have been a victorious British team, except for unfortunate questions over *Victory's* rating, which turned out to have been miscalculated to her advantage.

The late David May, a RLymYC Member and owner of the Berthon Boat Company, held six campaigns from 1971 to get into the British AC team. The first was *Winsome 2*, then *3* then *4*, *Winsome 77*, *Winsome Gold* and *Mayhem*, but David never quite made the team. Perversely his *Winsome 2* proved quick enough in the trials to be selected, but that year David chose not to join the team. I was his navigator in 1973 and 1975 in between naval sea appointments.

Yacht designers and Members of the Club Rob Humphreys and the late Ed Dubois both designed a number of AC successful yachts vying for the British team. Rob designed *Jade* in 1983 which nearly got in the team, and another *Jade* in 1985 which *did* get into the team and won the One Ton Cup that year. Larry and Debbie Woodell were her American owners and Club Members from 1992. I was the British team manager in 1985 but failed to fully unite the team, which probably had the fastest yachts. All three boats had professional skippers and crew for the first time and as such received bonus payments for *individual* boat results. Afterwards I realised I should have probably insisted that the boat should only be selected if win-bonuses were paid for a *whole team result* (i.e. for winning the Admiral's Cup), not individual races. Though Graham Walker's yacht with Harold Cudmore as skipper won individually overall and *Panda* won the Fastnet Race overall, the British team came second out of eighteen nations behind the German team.

Rob Humphreys designed *Juno 3* for Michael Peacock, Member of the Club from 1987, which not only got into the team in 1987 but won the Fastnet overall. He also designed a *Marionette* and, jointly with Ed Dubois, *Pocket Battleship*. The second *Jade*, renamed *Centurion Musclor*, was subsequently top boat in the French AC team which ended eighth nation overall.

Ed Dubois designed *Indulgence* and the Australian *Police Car*, the latter being top boat in the winning Aussie team of 1979 which managed to excel in the famous Fastnet storm. Later he designed *Full Pelt*, which was top boat in the Irish AC team of 1987, the Irish team coming fourth: their best ever result. He also designed *Winsome Gold*.

As Admiral's Cup results came in in the course of the series, everyone could see exactly what was going on through results displayed at the Groves and Gutteridge marina in Cowes where all the yachts were based. This was due to 'Brad's Board' – a most welcome feature before the days of the internet – designed, of course, by Jonathan Bradbeer who later became the Commodore of the RORC.

Graham Walker – RLymYC Member from 2011 – entered the AC fray in 1983. His first AC crew included Jonathan Bradbeer and myself. The boat was named *Indulgence*, as were nearly all Graham's yachts, and despite being selected for the British Team, turned out to be not particularly fast. The splendid 'flyers' she successfully took in the trials did not work out so well in the event itself. Graham was not discouraged and treated the matter as 'uncompleted business', entering another five Admiral's Cup campaigns, eventually achieving success. He ended up jointly owning *Phoenix* – the top individual AC series boat in 1985 – as, in the British selection trials, Graham's yacht *Indulgence* had struck the wreck of the *Empress Queen* on Bembridge Ledge and *sunk*! He and his crew were taken off in time and teamed up with Lloyd Bankson, whose similar boat was considered less likely to get in the team. Graham was in the team again in 1987, coming second, and was in the winning team in 1989. His boat was again selected in 1993, nearly equalling Robin Aisher's splendid record of four selections for the British team.

The Admiral's Cup has sadly had its day but, in the 70s and 80s, when so many nations took part from all over the world, the outcome was of intense worldwide interest and the lucky participants, quite a few from the Club, felt that they were making rich yachting history – as indeed they were. Indeed, the Royal Lymington Yacht Club had a strong association with the Admiral's Cup and achieved great success. ⚓

Eclipse going well along the Beaulieu shore in one of the 1979 Admiral's Cup inshore races. Phil Crebbin (Olympic bronze) is on the helm and Iain Macdonald-Smith (Olympic gold) is on the spinnaker sheet

19 Royal Lymington Cup – A Quarter of a Century of Matchless Racing.

Nick Ryley, past Royal Lymington Cup skipper, long time General Committee Member, racer and current Captain of Motorboats, provides a personal perspective of the creation and execution of the Royal Lymington Cup.

In 1974, the Rear Commodore Sailing, Eileen Caulcutt, wondered if Royal Lymington Yacht Club Members were prepared to jump off a cliff. It had just been suggested that it should run a match-racing regatta? What was that? Could the Club cope? Was it grabbing a nautical tiger by its tail?!

A very experienced sailor called Bill Green had just returned from visiting his family in California; whilst there he had come across a regatta called the Congressional Cup, which was known as a match-racing regatta. It was proving very popular: no handicaps, one against one, immediate results; coming first was everything and coming second was nothing. Bill thought the formula might work well at the Royal Lymington and could become a high-profile event if it succeeded.

The key need for the regatta was to have equal, identical boats, so that winning came down to the skill of the helm and his crew. No blaming your tools, except perhaps in the early years before the boats became really

*Close racing
Westerly Fulmars*

equal and new sails were provided. It was fortuitous that Bill Green worked for Contessa Yachts, run by Jeremy Rogers, and they were able to round up Contessa 32s to be the first fleet. There was a huge amount to learn about this arm of racing and the Club had to think on its feet.

The General Committee (at the time it was known as the Executive Committee) probably did not realise what it was letting itself in for and for how long it might go on! The event started at the right time in terms of sponsorship, organising talent in the Club membership and sailors wanting to race. As the event expanded both in size and quality and changed from a local to a world event, it shone a spotlight on all the different areas involved: the need for matched boats; pressure on the rules of racing; how to administer them on the water; finding funds so that foreign skippers and crews could get to the event; racing equipment for the Club; Race Officers who could run back-to-back racing for up to 108 races in a week. The event bought the first fax machine to the Club and a set of matched handheld VHFs for use on the water. Organising for the following year's event began before the start of the current year's, so that the skippers and crews had a date for their diaries. The winner of course had an automatic invite.

The first event in 1974 was a great success but rumour goes that it took so much out of the Club that it did not run again until 1976. At the same time, it was felt the regatta should have its own name rather than Congressional Cup, so it became the Royal Lymington Cup from then on. The logistics were formidable and took a while to settle down. Just imagine: in the regatta's heyday there were upwards of 150 volunteers involved, and the sponsorship sum for the World Championship 1989 was well into six figures.

The event would not have got off the ground without the Contessa 32s and then OOD 34s owners generously lending their boats. They or their representatives were invited on board to keep an eye on their investment. They crewed in the early days but differences in skill levels could lead to more inequality, and they took a back seat as the stakes increased. Once matched charter fleets came into use, the skippers only had their own crews and paid a refundable deposit to keep them somewhat under control whilst in combat.

Over the 25 years, seven different classes of boats were used. The first four years of the event used Jeremy Rogers' Contessa 32s: the obvious choice as so many Members owned and raced them. But despite being similar, there were differences in detailed fitting out and in performance; most of all, their sails came from several different makers. Top-class match racing demands equal boats. Therefore, in 1980, the new Rogers-built class of

Royal Lymington Cup match racing in the 90's

Vauxhall Royal Lymington Cup

CRUISING

Hard to believe that this year was the 20th Royal Lymington Cup - but it was, and at a special party a gathering of the Old and Bold of the event brought the likes of Eileen (Canlcut/Elliot) and Harold Cudmore from distant parts (well, Cowes, actually) to join winners, helpers and Jurors (it wasn't always on-the-water umpiring) from bygone days. What was significant was not how many but how few guests there were who had not already been around all week, running this year's event. The R Lym Cup really is 'Our Lym Cup', and the enthusiasm for the event brings the enormous race team back year after year.

As to the regatta itself, club sponsorship manager/negotiator/brinksman Ken Robinson brought to us one of the best sponsors to date: Vauxhall, who just happened to make a car called the Omega which is rather handy since the world circuit is sponsored by the watch manufacturer of that name. There's synergy for you. If Ken were a sky-diver, he would hold the world record for delayed-opening jumps. He would probably hold the record for the highest bounce, as well: the Vauxhall deal was cut to a schedule that made even the eleventh-hour deal with the Sports Aid Foundation in 1993 looked relaxed.

Much earlier - indeed, in 1993 - another sponsor had actually approached us and arrangements were well in hand when the continued recession in Europe had slowed the train of events to a snail's pace. When the deal not so much fell through as merely did not happen, we planned the event on a no-sponsorship profile. Contrary to popular belief outside our club, a major match race regatta can take place without sponsorship as we have already demonstrated - but one runs a better event, with a higher profile, when a sponsor is

involved. Well done Ken. Again.

An innovation this year was to hold an international qualifying tournament before the Vauxhall Royal Lymington Cup itself, to which came not merely young hopefuls keen to have a go at the Big Names, but some of the Big Names themselves, who for whatever reason could not be invited straight into the main event. (Because ours is the principal international match race event in Britain - the only so-called Grade One regatta - there are funny rules about who should and should not get invitations. For a full explanation of the workings of the world match race ranking system and how the invitation system operates, approach Ken Robinson or Nick Ryley in the bar, making sure you have a pocketful of silver. Both drink Ringwood, and it takes a long time.) Suffice it to say that this idea was not merely a success within our own walls, but was widely acclaimed both by competitors and in the yachting and the daily press (including some which hadn't been written either by Malcolm McKeag or Bob Fisher). Two skippers qualified this way for the main event, and gratifyingly each then went as far as the semi-final.

The final was drawn between Chris Law, a long-time competitor who had never quite won, and Thierry Pepponet, of France. It went all the way to five matches in a first-to-win-three final with Law eventually winning 3-2.

Malcolm McKeag
Rear Commodore
Sailing

I can remember thinking at the St Malo meet, whilst wrapped in full thermals, that two weeks of sun would have everyone saying what a good summer we were having. The weather at the time certainly gave no indication that we would have the finest summer for some years. It certainly helped to make our mid summer and St Vaast meets enjoyable.

There is an article elsewhere on sailing for the disabled, but I cannot let this opportunity go without saying thank you to all those involved in making these cruises such a success. One only has to see the thank you letters to realise how very worthwhile the events are; further volunteers to help afloat or ashore are always welcome.

The Needles Relief will take place as planned on Saturday 17th December. Unfortunately it seems that the light will not be manned at the time, the keepers having left on December 7th, so we shall be watching the RNLI doing an exercise in the Western Solent. The usual party in Yarmouth will follow. Details in the chart room.

Subject to sufficient numbers there will again be an opportunity for those who wish to take an SSB radio course and examination some time in February. A VHF one day course and examination will also be on offer. Further details are in the chart room.

Finally, I would mention that suggestions and volunteers for next year's lecture programme are always welcome.

James Beattie
Captain of Cruising

Pottership from Autumn 1994 covers the Royal Lymington Cup. (Pottership back-copies are available on the Club website)

Offshore One Design 34s was adopted – all very recently launched with a requirement to be equal. Being privately owned did mean that the boats had to be stripped before the event and reassembled afterwards, a hard job that was masterminded with aplomb by Roger Hawkes and his team. In 1985 we were able to attract charter companies to lend their fleets because of the exposure the event was receiving. The first boats were Westerly Fulmars, followed by the Beneteau First Europe used in 1989 for the World Championship at Lymington. Then Sunsail came on board with Beneteau 35S5s and Jeanneau Sunfast 30s. In 1995 the RYA was supporting a Match Racing programme of its own and had acquired a fleet of Beneteau First Class 8s which were set up to race; they provided very good racing until the finale in 1999. If a skipper asked, 'Can I change something on my boat' the answer was 'No' before he'd even stopped speaking!

As the skippers became more professional and prize money and world rankings were introduced, the equality of the boats became an imperative for the event.

The Royal Lymington Cup began to inspire international reporting, and our reputation for superbly organised world-class racing in equal boats grew with it. This marked the transition of the event from a domestic regatta with one or two overseas 'guest skippers' to a truly international event, recognised worldwide. The press boat *Cygnet*, loaned by Lord Montague of Beaulieu and helmed by Ken Robinson, became the yachting journalist platform and communications hub, with reports going out worldwide. It was a well-oiled machine!

The main Event Committee never comprised much more than seven people, with each running a sub-committee as required. Over the 25 years there were only three Chairpersons: firstly Eileen Caulcutt – who really made it what it became – Nick Ryley and Tony Blachford. The names of those who served the regatta are legion but, in particular, I should mention: Ken Robinson who conjured huge amounts of sponsorship from thin air; Elsa Green who found beds for the crews and fended off the women folk competing for their attention; Roger Hawkes, who had the hard job of looking after the boats and appeasing picky skippers; Bryan Willis and John Doerr on the umpiring side; and finally Jonathan Hutchinson, the Secretary of the time who had to keep the Club from being swamped. In fact he also became a stalwart of the Race Committee, plotting buoy positions and running four VHFs at once to keep things on the right track. What became apparent over these 25 years was the trust and the reliance between members on the committee, so that each year the event became better and better. The Club Members rallied around to an extraordinary extent and there were always volunteers to assist with the needs of the event. Even now in 2022, Royal Lymington Cup shirts in various colours and with different logos can be seen around the town.

The registration office was the centre of attention on the first day as fit crews from around the world stripped down to the altogether to make the weight limit. Ably handled by the ever-alert Rachel Nuding and Annie Littlejohn, on one occasion a huge New Zealander was carrying his weight with fingers curled on the picture rail whilst everyone else read the weighing machine. He did not get away with it and all the crew had to drop a few pounds to get down to weight. One crew from Canada misread the weight completely and spent time in the sauna, running in wetsuits and taking diuretics; they made the weight but were so weakened they did not sail well. This illustrates the development of the event: the next year a drugs rule was introduced to make sure that weight loss was achieved naturally.

We had the very best yacht-racing administrators – especially Mary Pera on the racing rules and Protest Committee Chair; and Eileen Caulcutt on race management – and the very best international judges.

The race team, organised by Sally Potter-Kalis, went from club racing to being the best in the game. Try organising 108 races in 5 days, with the races having proper windward–leeward legs. Match racing does not work with only reaching legs, so the course had to be altered to take account of the vagaries of the wind; also of course, do not forget the tide. The event bought VHFs for the Club so the event RIBs could report back in real time the wind and direction at the different buoys, or further to windward when sent as a 'wind finder'. Nick Potter was a master at race management and Tony

Below and opposite: Dick Deaver close tacking covering opposition

Blachford at course plotting. Members who learnt the ropes on the Cup race teams have worked on Race Committees at the Olympics, the America's Cup, Caribbean and Mediterranean regattas and for the RORC. This legacy has lasted, so the Club still enjoys high-level race management.

The first helmsmen were well known skippers from the UK and Ireland; they brought their own crews, normally people they crewed with regularly and who had the requisite skills. The racing was so close that it quickly became apparent that a poor start could decide the race, or one slip in boat handling could put a crew behind. It became a training ground for top-class crews aiming for the America's Cup, but more on that later.

As the event gathered momentum, the net was cast wider for skippers; in 1978 Pelle Petersen from Sweden came and, the following year, two Americans crossed from California. Dick Deaver won both the Royal Lymington Cup and the Congressional Cup in the same year. The pace was hotting up; other events began to appear whose winners were invited, and competitive skippers were not shy in contacting the Royal Lymington.

The 25 years that the event ran saw 266 entrants to skipper: about 1,350 sailors altogether if you take an average of five crew. Some years the boats being used took more crews than others. There were obviously skippers and crews from the UK but also Eire, Sweden, USA, France, Australia, Italy, Canada, New Zealand, Norway, Germany, South Africa, Japan, the Netherlands, Puerto Rico, Spain, Finland, Brazil, Russia, Hong Kong and Croatia. The Royal Lymington can certainly lay claim to running International events with a capital 'I'.

The quality of the sailors is very interesting. If one takes the America's Cup as the pinnacle of yacht racing, John Bertrand from Australia, the first to take the Cup away from the Americans, also won the Royal Lymington Cup in the same year, 1983. David Barnes of New Zealand won the Old Mug in 1988 and the American Ed Baird in 2007. Perhaps the most well-known is Russell Coutts, who has won the America's Cup three times but did not manage to win the Royal Lymington Cup! Do not think that these were the only America's Cup sailors we entertained that took part at Lymington. Probably about 50 per cent of the skippers and crews were involved in the America's Cup at one time or another. The competitive racing allowing them to hone their skills; in fact, experienced match racers are prized on racing boats as they are used to close-quarters sailing. Skippers can win, but not without excellent crews, and many people who cut their teeth in the Cup went on to great things.

Club Member Ian Williams is the leading match racer in the world today, having won six World Championships, but he cut his teeth at Lymington. Club Members who took part as skippers in the event are Peter Schofield, David May, Chris Law, Jeremy Rogers, George Tinley, John McCarthy, Peter Bruce, Andrew Hurst, Titch Blachford, Ben Vines, Ian Williams and Nick Ryley.

The speed at which the event expanded was among the many factors that created tensions among Members in 1987–9. There was a tendency for the more reactionary Members to state 'What the Members think is...' without actually having any idea, as they were out of touch with the changing attitudes and realities of the time. Ken Robinson's consultancy researched public opinions and attitudes, and proposed (at no cost to the Club) a survey of all Members to ascertain their views. The results helped quell unrest and demonstrated the majority's enthusiasm for the event ,and what it added to the Club in terms of prestige, skill levels and presence in the marine world. It also promoted a realistic attitude to the acceptance of sponsorship, which has served the Club well over the years.

The 'on water activities' tend to take centre stage but the 'off the water' aspects of the event were as important. The morning pre-race briefings with coffee in hand, weather reports, head-masterly notices to errant competitors and especially the event dinners and prize giving were really memorable – for competitors, the core team, and the many volunteers. Several of the leading international skippers and their crews would be hosted year after year by the same Members, whose houses became the international team HQ for the event. Iain Murray, who was with Ken and Jo Robinson, referred to Beaulieu as 'the car yard'. As it happens, Iain went on to be the Regatta Director for the America's Cup.

Times change but a hurdle in the 1980s was to agree an invite to a Japanese sailor when some Members had served on the Thailand–Burma railway during the Second World War. Fortunately, it was understood that times had moved on and Makoto Namba proved a popular skipper.

Times were changing on the water too and coming to grips with the way the racing rules were being used did not happen overnight. The racing world at that time was used to hoisting a red flag, writing out a script of their view of an incident, delivering their version in front of a panel of three experts and then, after much debate and deliberation by the Protest Committee, finally a verdict. Sometimes the protests (and they were often numerous), went on till midnight. This did not sit well with the fast and furious pace of the match-racing scene; the protests in this form interrupted the programme, and with so many races in a day, it was tiring on the crews when they came ashore. One famous protest was filmed and shown live as it happened in the room above where the protest was taking place. When the crowd above disagreed with a skipper's version of the events, they stamped on the floor. The ceiling had been freshly painted white and the skippers, film makers and Committee found themselves in a blizzard of paint flakes. It was a protest involving Harold Cudmore! A further problem was that many of the traditional members of Protest Committees were not up to date with the close racing prevalent in this arm of the sport. A trial was run with independent observers for the Protest Committee on the back of competitors' boats. Health and Safety would have had a seizure if they had seen them hanging on the pushpit as boats just missed on a port and starboard.

The first umpiring on the water happened in 1992 in the USA and was quickly taken up at Lymington. Bryan Willis, the then Chief Umpire, was an enthusiast and helped to create the umpiring rule book at Lymington which was then taken on by John Doerr. Over the next few years umpiring on the water from RIBs and the addition of a wing boat, to advise on overlaps, became the norm, with immediate decisions improving the running of the regatta. The 270-degree turn penalty was suggested by Tony Blachford and became the norm: enough of a set-back, but not one that removed the chance of a comeback. Another innovation that other sports would do well to take up was that after racing, an umpires' and skippers' forum discussed the day's decisions: not to overturn them but so all involved could understand the problems in making these decisions in a fast-moving scene, often in tough weather. Now in the America's Cup there are no umpires on the water: they apparently sit in a booth surrounded by screens and judge from there. How exciting!

With loaned boats and volunteers, the main costs were fuel, matching sails and some food, but to attract skippers from afar, prize money was needed. That meant sponsors and they in turn understandably wanted press coverage. So, from being quite cheap to run, the costs could escalate exponentially, particularly if helicopters were involved for filming. Ken Robinson was the mastermind behind the fund raising, and over the years household names such as Vauxhall, Duracell, Long-life Beer, Dunhill, Brut by Faberge, Hoya, Westerly Yachts, Mazda, Sunsail, Renaissance Insurance and even Wightlink put their name to the event. The sponsor fees had to cover the ever-rising costs of this branding, as from year to year the event became more organisationally sophisticated in every way, both ashore and afloat. It could never run at a loss, so the plan was always to have a small surplus. This was a safeguard, but also allowed the Club to benefit on occasion.

By the late 1980s, the Royal Lymington Cup was generally considered to be the pre-eminent match-racing regatta worldwide – and a cooperative network had evolved between the leading clubs worldwide over all aspects of the management of these regattas. Skippers, their core crew members and some top officials travelled from event to event, sequenced to avoid clashes, leading up to each America's Cup or the Olympics. In 1985, at the instigation of the Long Beach Yacht Club, a standing conference was formed, named the World Match Racing Conference (WMRC). In the pre-internet days, delegates met internationally at events, or in New York. Eileen Caulcutt, the much-respected Member, was the only lady present. Ken Robinson attended the earliest meetings to talk to WMRC about how they might raise enough funding to cover the costs of a top-class World Championship final regatta each year, and to contribute to the costs of all the WMRC members' events. Ken convinced the WMRC that this was viable and was 'volunteered' to approach the world's top sports marketing organisation, Mark McCormack's

International Management Group (IMG). After tough negotiations he managed to persuade them to buy the sponsorship rights to the World Championship of Match-Race Sailing for $500,000. This funded the Championship for several years and ensured TV coverage, as IMG had recently established TransWorld Sport and wanted to cover sailing, with Gary Jobson as their presenter. Subsequently through these arrangements IMG contracted the World Championship to Mazda, who they represented, and Ken managed to sign up Omega to sponsor the Royal Lymington Cup.

It was against this background that the Royal Lymington Yacht Club staged probably its finest match-racing event, the culmination of the annual series of WMRC member regattas, the World Championship in 1989, a truly great event in the Club's yacht-racing history. Comparing all the member events worldwide, it can be said without hesitation that the Royal Lymington Yacht Club's impeccable organisation, yacht-racing expertise and unrivalled hospitality was exemplary and was commented on by other clubs. But the events fed off each other's experiences, and all the WMRC regattas benefitted. There was a marquee in the park with a covered walkway to the Club, the town was in bloom and VIPs from the sailing world and other regattas all attended. Peter Gilmore went round the last mark in the last race and only had to finish to be World Champion, but his crew did not pull on the backstay fast enough and the rig and foredeck hand went over the bow into the water. Chris Dickson sailed on to be 1989 World Champion. All on film.

Ask any Member who was involved and they will say that their involvement in the Royal Lymington Cup is a shining memory of all that is best in this fine Club. It required knowledge, skill, commitment and cutting-edge competence in the organisation and conduct of yacht racing at the highest level of world sailing. The event was dependent on the hard work, expertise and generosity of Members who were involved in staging each regatta. The camaraderie that ensued strengthened the heart of the Club and our activities both afloat and in the Clubhouse. ⊗

20 Race Management

Tony Blatchford, himself a stalwart of our race management programme, on how our Club gained its acknowledged reputation as a leader in its field.

Lymington was regarded as a backwater for competitive racing until the mid-1970s. Local racing in XODs and Fireflys was very competitive, but the relatively strong current reduced the racing window, as there was often too little wind to get over the ground or large waves and strong winds when the tide went the other way.

However, things changed when Californian Bill Green persuaded the Club to hold an event based on the Congressional Cup created by the Long Beach Yacht Club in the mid-1960s: the format was two identical boats racing supplied by the organisers, on a windward/leeward course. The winner was the skipper who had the most points, having raced each other twice. This led to the Royal Lymington Cup which started in 1974 with some of the best British sailors, but which gained momentum in 1978 when the first overseas sailors were invited. A problem was that with the boats in such close contact, there were inevitably numerous protests which were held ashore after racing, and sometimes lasted well into the night, so the day's results were not known until the following morning.

Lymington was at the forefront of introducing onboard observers and instant penalties, meaning that the first over the line was the winner.

Over its 25 years most of the best sailors in the world were invited,

including most of the America's Cup winners. Match racing was very popular throughout the world and many other countries followed the format The highlight was in 1989 when the Club hosted the World Championship, which involved around 130 Club volunteers. The Congressional Cup and Lymington were the only tournaments not to offer prize money. As time went on, costs increased significantly as boats had to be equalised and spares found for

*Race team on the
Club workboat*

everything. We were very fortunate in having Ken Robinson, the man with the magic purse, who was well enough connected to persuade sponsors to part with large sums of money to keep the show on the road. Despite lack of prize money, the Royal Lymington Cup was regarded as the best organised event on the World Tour

Our Patron The Princess Royal regularly visited and often followed the racing in an umpire boat. On one occasion, she was transferring from the Committee Boat to the umpire RIB and the chief umpire (no name but he had a beard and gives rules lectures) was so intent on making sure that she was comfortable that he ran headlong into the press boat, depositing all three in the RIB into six inches of bilge water. I don't believe any of the photos were published! At the turn of the century, racing was becoming professional with indecent sums of money involved, so we decided to 'quit while we were ahead' and let the Cup rest at the top of the Club stairs.

The match-racing circuit is very competitive and can now be very lucrative. Joining is by invitation only. In the 1980s Club Member Phil Crebbin, Olympic medallist and previous winner of our event, kindly donated a trophy for a series to be held on the weekend before the main event, with the winner gaining an entry to the event itself. The other way is through determination: in 1998 I had a phone call from the father of James Spithill in Australia, asking if we would invite his son. He was lucky in that we had just received a withdrawal, so he was able to take the final place. Almost all sailors know where it went from there, with the America's Cup being the ultimate reward.

Club Member Ian Williams fights for the top spot each year and has been world number one on many occasions.

In the mid 1990s, the RYA purchased its own fleet of Beneteau First Class 8s, primarily to increase the opportunities for sailors to gain match-racing experience, particularly as the discipline had been chosen for future Olympics.

We used these boats a few times at the Royal Lymington Cup and were the logical choice to run the first few national championships, which proved a great success.

The Club is fortunate in having a relatively large pool of qualified race officers to cope with the busy programme. It is often said that to be a successful race officer, it helps to be a successful racer. It is useful to imagine yourself in one of the boats and think 'Which end of the line would I start? Which side of the course would I take?' In tidal conditions this is much safer than relying on charts and maths. On one occasion, while sharing the West Solent with one of the senior central clubs, who relied entirely on Admiralty charts for course setting, we were monitoring their radio traffic, to hear 'If you lay the windward mark on those co-ordinates, it will be right in the middle of the RLymYC's committee boats cockpit! Shall we have a rethink?'

Domestically the XOD Class continues to thrive, with its own dedicated team of race officers, who also very kindly look after the ever-growing Folkboat fleet, which is much appreciated.

In the 1990s, we ran several training regattas for potential members of the British Blind Sailing Team, for the World Championships in Perth, Australia. We were even honoured with the attendance of The Princess Royal, who happens also to be the Patron of RYA Sailability. The effort was worthwhile, as the team returned with two out of three gold medals, with two Club Members being part of the winning crew. The Club was also asked to provide the entire race management team, Committee Boat and all, for the following Worlds at the RYA Centre in Portland.

Big boat racing took off at the Club during the middle part of the Admiral's Cup when we were asked by the Royal Ocean Racing Club to run the inshore races of the event. This led on to us running a pre-AC

Race Officer Malcolm McKeag aboard Chinook

Race Officer Simon Van Der Byl prepares for racing

event in conjunction with Berthon and Source as a practice for the event, and to give those who didn't make their national teams a chance to have some fun and maybe prove a point to their selectors! This proved a great success with up to 50 entries and showed a lot of mid-Solent boat owners that the West Solent was not such a bad place to enjoy some good racing.

We are very fortunate in having Christchurch Bay on our doorstep, because here the sea breeze sets in earlier, and the relatively weak current is quite even across the course area. Access to the Bay has allowed us to undertake ambitious and prestigious projects, such as the Etchells World Championship, Sigma 38, J 109, SB3 (now known as SB20), Contessa 32, and J80 Nationals, to name but a few. If the conditions aren't suitable, we always have our usual patch to fall back on, despite one Swedish competitor saying, 'It's like sailing on a river!'

The four Member umpires at one of the seminars, left to right, Mike, John, Malcolm and Gordon.

John Doerr has been awarded one of the most prestigious rôles in yacht racing. He has been ap......

Early in 1988 this Club, and in particular Eileen Caulcut, Nick Ryley and Tony Blachford, committed the RLymYC to using umpires. This provided John with his first......

Autumn 1994
Pottership reports John Doerr appointed chief umpire and chairman of the International Jury for the XXIV Americas Cup. With him are three other international umpires: Mike Urwin, Malcolm McKeag and Gordon Stredwick – RLymYC had 4 of the 5 UK Umpires at that time

Our domestic racing is thriving, with Thursday Evening Racing well supported for many years and much enjoyed, thanks to the long suffering and dedicated race team, who are always first out and last back. A few will remember that this series was originally Wednesday afternoon cruiser racing about 50 years ago! It has been necessary for safety reasons for all Thursday Racing to finish at the end of the river. Many will remember the wonderful sight of all the colourful spinnakers crossing the Club line and rushing to clear everything up before they ran out of room! And the Race Team got home first!

Racing is ever changing, in some cases for no apparent reason. For example, the season long Solent Points Championship, which was shared by most of the Solent clubs coming to Lymington at the end of the season, attracted around 150 entries. The extremely successful MacNamara Bowl, an event for all-female crews. ran for many years, but then numbers dropped and made the event unviable: one can only assume that owners were increasingly reluctant to loan their boats owing to insurance difficulties.

Races are also getting shorter – a match race used to be around 45 minutes long: it's now 15 to 20. A keelboat race used to be two hours, now one hour is the norm, and an RORC offshore race started on Friday evening, and you would often struggle to get to work on Monday; now it's likely to be about 24 hours. There is now a professional circuit where big money is to be made. Foiling is the biggest change: you now have to choose whether you wish to float or fly!

21 The Origins of the Club Starting Platform

Anyone crossing the Club start line at the Platform or just sailed by, leaving or returning to the river, may have wondered what and when were the origins of the Club's Starting Platform. Club Historian Graham Clark pondered these notions but could find no one who had any recollection of them, so started some digging of his own...

Conventional land maps are notoriously unreliable regarding the details of estuaries and especially the inter-tidal zone, between the lowest low water and the top of what is left of the marshes. Some say they could recall being able to walk out to the Platform – but why would such a structure be placed so close to the marsh? Others infer the whereabouts of HW and LW marks from the shading on maps (and even some charts), but the only reliable evidence is from old photographs, particularly aerial ones.

This rather indistinct view down the estuary to the Starting Platform, with the Club discernible on the right, dates from the late 1940s. The mud flats in the upper reaches of the river suggest it is not much above low water. Even then, the Platform is way out from the water's edge, so pre-war memories of walking out to it might be a little inaccurate

Photo credit: Paul French

Early in its existence, the Club was preoccupied with its own creation and that of its Clubhouse, but it would not have taken many years before its level of activity justified something as grand as having its own Starting Platform, but not until the 1930s, most likely. The research started in earnest with the Club's own archives, but these really only exist (or at least, those that the Club possesses) from the post-war period.

From old Club bulletins, which recorded an outline of all the doings of the Club, one can pick up references to the Platform being in considerable need of renovation after the war. Hardly surprising, given that it would have had no attention during the conflict, but at least that indicated the structure existed in the 1930s. But when? And did the Club build it, or acquire it, as it had done the Clubhouse?

Research then went in the direction of the UK Hydrographic Office. Surely they would have explicit details of the Platform's arrival and its purpose? The initial answer wasn't promising: no such structure existed on the 1895 Chart of the Western Solent, but it did in 1965... so it must have been built sometime between the two. Further delving, and with a little encouragement (but not so much as might elicit a bill for their labours), the Hydrographic Office went that extra mile (or at least several cables).

The UKHO provided extracts of the two charts (which, of course, were useless for detecting changes in the 1930s) of 1895 and 1965, but the absolute golden nugget was found in a unique and antiquated working document: the manuscript log of chart corrections for the area. From 1928 to 1946, the pages provided the most promising period when the Club might have created the structure. No evidence was found of a previously existing structure, so attention focused on the detailed entries of chart corrections

The Platform in all its modern glory, manned and fulfilling its function as the Club's offshore base for starting (and finishing) races

CELEBRATING THE CENTENARY

in the 30s. Amidst the myriad and detailed items – almost Dickensian in their recording – were two small line items, which are permitted to be copied here and to reside in the Club's archive:

Extract from the Corrections Ledger of the UK Hydrographic Office – file ref: NMR 5-1-2040 Solent (NM Ledger in 1940s) – reproduced with UKHO permission

Page identity: 2040 [the Admiralty Chart reference for Western Solent] – with columns thus:

Engraver Sent	Ret'd	Chart dated	CORRECTION	Authority for Correction	Cancel or N.M.

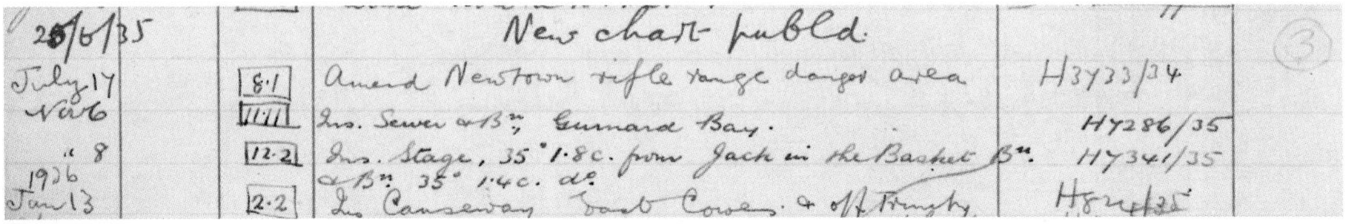

Extract from the Corrections Ledger of the UK Hydrographic Office – file ref: NMR 5-1-2040 Solent (NM Ledger in 1940s)

Reproduced with UKHO permission

From which it may be interpreted that from the new chart, published on 25 June 1935, the subsequent corrections were logged, on 8 November 1935:

12.2 Insert Stage, bearing 35deg, 1.8 chains distant from Jack in the Basket Beacon;

& Beacon, bearing 35deg, 1.4 chains distant from Jack in the Basket Beacon.

The authority being: H7341/35

Viewing the later, 1965, chart, the Platform is referred to as a 'stage' (defining the structure rather than its purpose), together with its off-lying distance mark – both having diamond marks, confirming their racing pedigree. The stage gave its name to the adjacent No.1 post, then also called 'Stage Boom'.

So, the quest is ended: the Starting Platform was built in 1935 for racing duties; it has been a Club feature for over 85 years. ✪

200

22 Cruising 1946–1967

Reference to cruising appear in all past bulletins produced by the Club. Below are a few taken between 1946 and 1967 which illustrate the gradual normalisation of cruising after the Second World War. In many respects they could have been taken from any decade from then up to the present day.

1946 The RLYC burgee has been flown in most of the ports on either side of the Channel during the 'summer'.

1948 Humphrey Barton gave a delightful talk on his cruising experiences in all sorts of boats from 14ft dinghies to 20 tonners. The several slides he showed of his own boat on the mud did him less than justice, but behind his modesty there was clearly a wealth of experience.

1950 With the improvement in the food situation in this country, the urge to go to France has not been quite so marked this year; nevertheless, it has been a rare day when the Yellow Flag has not been seen flying in the river.

1953 The winning log sailing under our colours for the Cadiz Cup showed skill and determination in sailing a 5-ton yacht a big distance into the Bay of Biscay and back in a very short time, and with a 'light' crew.

1957 Cross-Channel cruises have been a regular feature of the season,

*Nigel Lang's
Westerly Griffin,
Salty, homeward
bound*

and the weather encountered was on the whole much better than in 1956, particularly in the early part of the summer. Further afield Mr Peter Edwards has been voyaging in *Selamat* and Mr W. H. Farr and his family have been cruising in Scandinavian waters in *Penlena*.

A notable cruise was that of *Minion*, a 21ft 6in fin-keel sloop, converted from a day cruiser and sailed by David and John Giles, aged 22. They sailed across the Channel and were away for about 14 days. It was the first occasion on which these two young men had sailed abroad and they did some good passages in adverse weather conditions.

1958 The Commodore (J. R. Bryans) was a popular winner of the Cadiz Cup for his Scandinavian Cruise. Colin McMullen did an outstanding voyage, much of it single-handed, round Britain. Robert Pretty, in his lovely new *Riwaru* had an enjoyable month's cruise to Holland and Mac Reynolds' *Free Trader* and Micky Armelin's *Menina* have also done some cross-Channel trips.

1960 *Riwaru* (Robert Pretty) sailed for the Caribbean in October. All Members wish him luck in this long cruise. Apart from this, the longest cruise is probably the Commodore's voyage to Marstrand and then home through the Little Belt and the Kiel Canal. Other shorter voyages were Colin McMullen's to the Biscay Ports in *Alexa* and the Pococks (Mike and Patricia) in their *Minion* to Brittany which won for them the Cadiz Cup – a fine effort by these two young people.

1961 When writing last year, Robert Pretty in *Riwaru* had just set sail for the Spanish Main and had reached Las Palmas. She reached the West Indies and spent the winter cruising in those waters.

1962 The Commodore in *Cheemaun* had a very good cruise to La Rochelle and Christopher Biddle took *Winkle* to Holland and the Baltic.

Simon Baddeley (aged 20) with Christopher Jameson did a very fine cruise in the five-tonner *Danica* from Lymington to Athens and back via the French canals. They were away about five months for which they won the Cadiz Cup.

1963 No one seems to be talking much about their cruises this year. Perhaps the weather had something to do with it. However, there were three entries for the Cadiz Cup, an improvement on the last few years. The trophy was

Powerboats like being *there* but it does not stop them enjoying getting there.

awarded to Simon Baddeley for a very fine account of a single-handed cruise to the Normandy Coast in his two-and-half-ton Hillard sloop, *Two Pearls*.

1964 It was good to see 'Hum' Barton in the Club again after a considerable absence in foreign parts. He spent several weeks in Lymington following a transatlantic crossing from Halifax in 21 days. He left for his seventh transatlantic crossing bound for the Caribbean.

Four logs were entered for the Cadiz Cup which was won by a very fine account of a cruise by C. D. Dawson's *Ayesha* from Cork to Lymington via the north and west coasts of Brittany. The unusual feature of this cruise was that it was done in very light weather, in the old-fashioned way, without the use of an engine.

1965 The miserable weather must have disheartened the cruising enthusiasts. Not a single log was submitted for the Cadiz Cup. However, two of the Flag Officers set a good example. The Commodore was away for ten weeks in *Tamarack* and spent a considerable time in Danish waters, and had a lot of fun in the Dutch and German canals. The weather, he reports, was no better there. Rear Commodore Chris Bowen in the Laurent Giles' Peter Duck *Pomerol* did an extensive cruise in Dutch waters.

1967 There were five entries for the Cadiz Cup this year, covering such cruises as *Cheemaun*'s voyage around Ireland, Bob Nock's trip to Cherbourg and Alderney in his new motor yacht *Heather*, Noel Bond-Williams Mediterranean cruise in *Bowstring*, Colonel Landon's cruise under sail to the Rias of north-west Spain and Mike Pocock's voyage across the Atlantic from the West Indies in Humphrey Barton's *Rose Rambler*. The judges were unanimous in awarding the Cup to *Rose Rambler* as being the most outstanding achievement.

23 RLymYC Circumnavigators

Many cruising sailors dream of making a circumnavigation. Very few of those actually get away, and of those who do, maybe half fail to complete the voyage. It's a daunting prospect and usually a pretty challenging experience too. Since 1977 some 27 cruising Members of the RLymYC are known to have completed their circuit of the globe. Full descriptions of their voyages are posted on the Club's website. Regretfully, it has proved impossible to accommodate all their exploits in this book. Below are all-too-brief details of their voyage(s).

CIRCUMNAVIGATORS – DETAILS

CREW	BOAT	DATES & ROUTE
Naomi James	Express Crusader (*Spirit of Cutty Sark*) – Gallant 53	Departed Dartmouth on 9 September 1977. Route – Clipper Ship, 3 Great Capes, Falkland Islands, completed 8 June 1978 at Dartmouth. 'The unavoidable port calls negated the chance of a non-stop (solo) record. I did beat Francis Chichester's time for a single-handed circumnavigation – but he stopped in Australia for some weeks. Nevertheless, the sense of achievement and self-discovery resulting from a nine-month sea voyage was life changing, as all who undertake such journeys discover.'

Donald Begg	*Lydia* – Bowman 48	Sailed from Lymington for the West Indies on 15 September 2014, and from there westwards on 9 January 2016; completed my circumnavigation Grenada to Grenada on 21 March 2019; positioned the boat in the BVI ready for the final transatlantic home in February 2020; was then defeated by the Coronavirus lockdown, had the boat transported to Southampton on a steamer, and arrived back in Lymington on 25 June 2020.
Nicholas & Sally Davies	*Liemba* – Nicholson 35	Departed from Lymington 9 September 1979, arrived back in Lymington 24 May 1986. Route:

Part 1: Lymington, Brittany, NW Spain, Portugal, Madeira, Canaries, Barbados, Tobago, Windward Isles, Leeward Isles, British and US Virgin Islands, San Blas Islands (Panama), Panama Canal, west coasts of Panama, Costa Rica and Mexico, San Diego (California).

Part 2: After my stay in San Diego, sailed direct to the Marquesas Islands, Tuamotu Islands, Tahiti, Leeward Islands of French Polynesia, Cook Islands, Tonga, Fiji, New Caledonia, Brisbane and Mooloolaba for the cyclone season and work.

Part 3: From Mooloolaba, up the east coast of Queensland, Torres Strait, Arnhem Land, Darwin, Bali, Christmas Island, Cocos Keeling Islands, Sri Lanka, Cochin (Kerala, India), Aden, Mocha (North Yemen), Sudan, Egypt, Suez Canal, Cyprus.

Part 4: From Larnaca to Turkey, Greek Aegean, Corinth Canal, Ionian Islands, Sicily, west coast of Italy and its islands, Elba, Corsica, south coast of France, French canals (Rhone, Saône, Burgundy, Yonne, Seine), Le Havre, and back to Lymington.

Alan & Penny Spriggs	*Pennypincher* – Oyster 46	Departed St Peter Port, Guernsey 18 October 1990. – Route Tradewinds. Gibraltar, Las Palmas, St Lucia, Panama, Galapagos, Marquesas, Tahiti, Bora Bora, Tonga, Fiji, Vanuatu, Australia, Bali, Singapore, Malaysia, Lankawi, Thailand, Sri Lanka, Djibouti, Sudan, Suez, Malta, Gibraltar. Completion on 20 May 1992 St Peter Port, Guernsey.
Mike & Pat Pocock	*Blackjack* – a 38-footer designed by Mike for Rodney Barton	Departed Lymington August 1987. Route – Caribbean, Panama, Alaska, Polynesia, Tonga, Fiji, Vanuatu, N.Z. Australia (Gladstone south about via Tasmania to Caernarvon), Chagos Is, Mauritius, Durban, Cape Town, St Helena, Bermuda, Caribbean, USA, arrived back in Lymington August 1994.
Charlie & Paula Tait	*Maia*	September 1993 – August 1996. Route – Trade wind circumnavigation via Panama, New Zealand, India, Suez, Med, French canal system.
Mike Thoyts	*Kinsa* – Rustler 36	Start: Chaguaramas, Trinidad, 28 February 1996. Route: Trinidad–Panama Canal–Marquesas–Fiji–New Zealand–New Caledonia–New Zealand–Australia–Mauritius–South Africa–St Helena–Cabedelo, Brazil –Trinidad. Finish Chaguaramas, Trinidad 11 November 1999.
Ian Tew	*Independent Freedom* – 13-ton Bermudan schooner 39 feet overall 32 feet on the waterline built by Freedom yachts in 1991	Start of Voyage Sandy Hook (20' South of New York) 10 October 1997. Route – New York, south to Delaware River, Chesapeake Canal, Chesapeake Bay, Newport, Intra Coastal Waterway, Fort Lauderdale. Nassau Bahamas. Commencement circumnavigation 18 December 1997 Cuba, Cayman Islands, Panama Canal, Galapagos Islands, Marquesas, Tuamotu, Tahiti, Tonga, New Zealand, New Caledonia, Bundaberg, Australia, Darwin, Bali, Singapore, Phuket Thailand, Galle Sri Lanka, Djibouti, Suez Canal, Ashkelon, Israel, Turkey, Malta, Tunisia, Gibraltar, Canary Islands, Cape Verde Islands, Antigua, Puerto Rico, Bahamas, Nassau Completed circumnavigation 25 March 2001. Bermuda, Azores, Beaulieu. End of voyage Tuesday 3 July 2001.

Ed & Genie Webb	*Wandering Dream* – Rival 38	Departed Lymington, August 2000. Route: Canaries, Caribbean, Panama Canal, Pacific (two years), Australasia, Indian Ocean, Cape of Good hope, St Helena, Ascension, Caribbean, Bermuda, Azores, UK. End in Lymington, August 2004
Phillip & Gillie Hutchinson	*Fenella* – Jeanneau Sun Odyssey 45	Left Gibraltar in September 2004. Route Gibraltar, Tenerife, San Blas Islands, Panama, Galapagos, Marquesas, Tahiti, Bora Bora, Tonga, Figi, Vanuatu, Australia, Western Timor, Bali, Singapore, Malaysia, Maldives, Djibouti, Egypt, Greece, Italy, Spain... arrived Gibraltar June 2007
Luke & Emma McEwan	*Eagle Wing* – Tradewind 35	Start: May 2003, Southsea (Langstone Harbour) Via: Falmouth, Galicia, Spain, Portugal, Porto Santo, Canaries, Guadeloupe, Dominica, St Lucia, St Vincent & The Grenadines, Grenada, Aruba, San Blas, Panama, Galapagos, Marquesas, Tuamotu, Society Islands, Suwarrow, Tonga, Australia, New Zealand, Tonga, Fiji, Vanuatu, New Caledonia, Australia, Christmas Island, Cocos Keeling, Chagos, Madagascar, Mozambique, South Africa, St Helena, Ascension Island, Tobago, Antigua & Barbuda, Azores, Salcombe. End: August 2007, Lymington
Hugh & Angela Farrant	*Spring Gold II* – Sadler Starlight 38	Departed Vilamoura (Portugal) 14 November 1998 and sailed to the Caribbean, (Grenada) and from there across the Caribbean to Panama, transited the Canal, out to the Galapagos, then across the Pacific calling into the Marquesas. We explored some of the Islands, then on to Tahiti from where we sailed to Rarotonga, then Nuie, and on to Tonga, exploring various islands in that group, then down to New Zealand where we kept the boat for over two years. Our return to the UK started in April 2002 sailing to Australia, Sydney, then up the East Coast and through to Darwin and then to Bali and on to Singapore. On to Phuket, where we were when the Tsunami arrived! Fortunately we were on the east side of the Island and were not really affected.

Then across the Indian Ocean to the Maldives, to Oman and up the Red
Sea through the Suez Canal and into the Mediterranean and to Turkey.
We berthed in Kemer Marina for two years and finally crossed the Med
and arrived back in Vilamoura 20 May 2009.

David & Annette Ridout	*Nordlys* – Swan 47	Start Lymington Sept 2000, finish Lymington June 2009 but actually crossed an outbound meridian in Tobago in April 2008. Route: Lymington, Lagos, Canaries, Cape Verdes, Antilles, Bermuda, Maine, Grand Manan (Canada), Maine, Massachusetts, RI, Connecticut, New Jersey, Delaware. Maryland (Chesapeake), Antilles, Venezuela, ABC islands, Colombia (Cartagena), San Blas, Panama, Galapagos, Marquesas, Tuamotus, French Polynesia, Penrhyn (Cook Islands), Tonga, New Zealand, Samoa, Wallis, Fiji, Vanuatu, New Zealand, Fiji, Vanuatu, Queensland Australia, Brisbane, Sydney, Hobart, south around Tasmania then up to Port Lincoln and across the Bight to Esperance and Fremantle, Christmas Island, Cocos, Chagos, Seychelles, Madagascar, South Africa, St Helena, Ascension, Tobago, Antilles. Bermuda, Azores, La Coruna, Dartmouth, Lymington.
Dick & Pam Moore	*Aliesha* – Halberg Rassy 36	Start on 25 June 2001 from Chichester Marina. - Route: Canaries; Caribbean; USA (Maine); Cuba, Panama Canal; Galapagos, Marquesas, Tuamotus, Society Islands, Tonga, Fiji, New Zealand; Fiji, Vanuatu, New Caledonia, Australia; Indonesia, Singapore, Malaysia, Thailand, Maldives, Oman, Yemen, Sudan, Egypt, Suez Canal, Turkey, Greece, Italy, France, Spain, Gibraltar, Azores, France and home. Completed 16 September 2010, in Chichester Marina.
Jeanne Socrates	*Nereida I* – Naiad 361	First Circumnavigation: Departed Zihuatanejo, Mexico, in March 2007. Route – the Marquesas, Tuamotus, Societies, Niue, Tonga, Fiji, Australia (Cairns to Darwin), Bali, Christmas Island, Cocos Keeling, Rodrigues, Mauritius, Reunion, S. Africa (Richards Bay to Cape Town),

Luderitz (Namibia), St Helena, Fernando de Noronha, Trinidad, Bonaire, Colon/Balboa (Panama Canal transit), Guatemala, Acapulco to half a day short of my end and starting point, Zihuatanejo, just 60 miles short of completion north of Acapulco, on 19 June 2008 when I lost my boat. I returned to Acapulco on Thursday 2 June 2016 and arrived in Zihuatanejo the following day, so completing this circumnavigation on Friday 3 June 2016.

Jeanne Socrates	*Nereida II* – Naiad 380	Second Circumnavigation: Departed Lanzarote October 2009, but as I headed down to S. Africa several rigging problems caused me to pull in to Cape Town for repairs. Being too late in the season to head back north to England and wanting to gain experience of the Southern Ocean, I eventually continued on east past Australia to New Zealand and then made for Vancouver from where I intended to start my next nonstop attempt. Cape Town 9 March 2010, Route – Nelson (N.Z.), Tahiti, Oahu and Kauai (Hawaii), Port Townsend (WA, USA), Vancouver and Victoria (B.C., Canada), nonstop to and around Cape Horn (knockdown), on to Ushuaia (Argentina), Stanley (Falklands), Victoria B.C. on 1 August 2012 having successfully rounded all five great capes on the way.
Jeanne Socrates	*Nereida II* – Naiad 380	Third Circumnavigation: Solo, nonstop, unassisted circumnavigation October 2012 – 8 July 2013 – becoming the oldest woman to achieve this.
Jeanne Socrates	*Nereida II* – Naiad 380	Fourth Circumnavigation: I expected to be at sea for seven to eight months (hopefully, faster than previously) but a surprising number of weather- and gear-related problems, many of them major, caused my journey to take just over 11 months to complete, not helped by damage caused by a knockdown off Stewart Island. Instead of arriving back by early June, I eventually made landfall on 7 September 2019,

despite a long catalogue of challenges which had needed to be overcome along the way in order to return to Victoria. This was my fourth solo circumnavigation and second successful nonstop one. I had become the oldest person to have sailed alone, nonstop and unassisted around the world via the Five Great Capes of the Southern Ocean.

John Andrews & Freda Haylett	*Qwyver* — Wauquiez 40 Pilot Saloon	Departed Lymington June 2007. Route: Portugal, Madeira, Canaries, Barbados, Trinidad & Tobago, Grenada and various Leeward and Windward Islands. Then to Los Roques, ABC Islands, Columbia (Cartagena & Islas Rosarios) San Blas Islands, Panama. Then Galapagos, Marquesas, Tuamotus, Society Islands, Isles Sou le Vent, Cook Islands, Niue, Tonga, New Zealand. On to Fiji, Vanuatu and Australia. Cocos Keeling Islands, Rodrigues, Mauritius and La Reunion before South Africa. Next ocean to Namibia, St Helena, Ascension and Cabedelo in Brazil, just north of Receife. Then to Kouru in French Guyana and back to Grenada which completed the circumnavigation. More Windward and Leewards then St Maarten, Bermuda and the Azores before arriving in Baltimore (the Irish one) and back to Lymington arriving in August 2013.
Colin and Sarah Seaman	*Moonbeam* — Oyster 55	Departed Fox's Marina in Ipswich on 5 October 2006 and returned to La Roche Bernard in Southern Brittany, which was to become our Home Port on 25 August 2012, 44,000nms later. We crossed our outbound track after five years and three months and 39,200nms. We followed the Trade Wind Route (as I had promised Sarah that we would only sail with the wind abaft the beam and in sunshine!) to New Zealand and returned home from Australia via South Africa. We had decided to abandon a plan to join the Blue Water Rally, routing to the Mediterranean because of the increased substantial threat of piracy that year. ⊗

24 The Club Today

Immediate past Vice Commodore John Tudor takes a look at where the Club is today and looks forward to the future.

Writing in 2022 we can look back with some satisfaction on 100 years of activity on the water, surviving two world wars and numerous economic challenges as well as weathering storms both literal and figurative, as well as the Covid epidemic. Yachting has evolved with the introduction of new materials and new designs, as well as changing social and leisure trends.

We look back on the foundation of the Club in 1922: growing membership (2,319 at the end of 2021), a new location for the Clubhouse to where we are today, the MacNamara Bowl, Royal Lymington Cup and hosting world class yachting, the introduction of Wednesday Junior Sailing as a community project, Thursday Evening Keelboats (every week running a regatta for around 80 boats during the season) and the growth in the number of classes sailed.

More recently, we have hired a Head Coach to make sure all our young sailors get the best training, not only to turn potential champions into winners but, crucially, to make sure more people enjoy their sailing. Not every young sailor can win an Olympic medal but we aim to make sure they can all enjoy sailing. Friday evening Junior Racing Series was conceived to achieve this and has grown from strength to strength in the last three years.

Opposite:
Colin and Sarah
Seaman's Oyster 55
Moonbeam

Overleaf:
Claire and Julian
Sowry, joint
Captains of Nordic
Folkboats in our
Centenary year,
round the needles
in Mistral, closely
watched by the RNLI

The Club is a hive of activity, with numerous teams of volunteers and staff preparing for events on and off the water. Sailing series, national and international events, RYA training courses, cruises, junior and youth coaching, Wednesday Junior Sailing, ladies sailing courses, lectures and talks, social events, open day, new Members' day, crew match and of course our Centenary celebrations – it's going to be an exciting year!

XODs (a class now in its 104th year), Folkboats, J80s, Scows, etc. all prove that a successful competitive design can offer great one-design sailing.

In 2021 we introduced a specific Motorboat section which now has 80+ members who explore both our local waters and further afield. We have also introduced stand-up paddle boards which we hope will prove an attraction for those who want to be on (or in!) the water, but not under sail or power.

We now have valued association with 38 reciprocal clubs worldwide which means our long-distance cruising sailors have friendly clubs as a home-from-home on their travels.

In the 2021 *Pottership* magazine, we reported the victory of Emily Mueller (and her crew Flo Brellisford) in the 29er Youth World Championship in Oman. Our youth sailors competed recently in the RYA Youth National Championships in North Wales. RLymYC sailors shone in double-handers: in the 29er Class winning First and Second overall and First mixed pair, and in the 420 Class winning First boys (Second overall). In the 29er Class a friendly battle for overall gold developed early on between RLymYC pair Ben Mueller / Sam Webb and fellow RLymYC Member Santi Sesto Cosby with crew Leo Wilkinson (Maidenhead SC). On the final day Santi and Leo were crowned RYA Youth National Champions with Ben and Sam finishing close behind in Silver. Meanwhile in the 420 Class, Henry Heathcote and Hector Bennett were First Boys (Second overall).

In April 2022, Club Member Ian Williams and the rest of team Gladstone's *Long Beach*, won the 57th edition of the prestigious Congressional Cup, securing Ian his 5th Crimson Blazer!

With so much going on, and so much success on the water, it is really invidious to pick out any one achievement, but perhaps the experience of Hattie Rogers is illustrative.

Hattie is one of the Lymington Rogers clan. Grandfather Jeremy, renowned for designing and building Contessas from his Lymington yards (now at the Lymington Yacht Haven), won the One Ton Cup and the Admiral's Cup and came second in the infamous 79 Fastnet race to name a few. Hattie's father Simon led the family crew to three overall victories in the Round The Island Race and class wins in the Fastnet amongst others. Brother Tom won two RYA National RIB Challenge trophies and, incidentally, with Simon helped build the Laser rack in the dinghy park.

Wednesday junior sailing – my first card completed – Hattie Rogers

Sir Ben Ainslie provides direction...

Hattie meanwhile graduated from Salterns SC to Wednesday Junior Sailing and then onto the RYA national pathway, winning many junior and youth trophies along the way.

Recently, getting ready to line up for the SailGP Inspire WASZP Grand Final in San Francisco, she received a surprise phone call asking her to step up to Ben Ainslie's Great Britain F50 SailGP Team. Having had the experience of a lifetime, she then appeared in the national press sailing with Ben, becoming 'fastest female helm' on the F50 SailGP circuit:

"Having grown up in Lymington, the Royal Lymington Yacht Club and the Wednesday Junior Sailing afternoon sessions played a major part of my childhood, as did the Salterns SC. I remember being so excited to get into my sailing kit and get on the water! It was always such a mad dash from Walhampton School on a Wednesday afternoon to make it in time for the four o'clock session. The doughnuts and the tea played an essential part, and all the volunteers were always so kind.

"It was this amazing foundation which then led me into the RYA national junior/ youth pathway from Oppies to 29ers, and gave me eight incredible years of racing, international travel and so much fun. Great friendships were forged with people from all over the world, many of whom I bump into on my travels today. When I started university, I then moved into single-handed foiling and bought a WASZP, and never looked back!

Hattie Rogers flying her Waszp, before winning the Inspire Racing x WASZP series in San Francisco

AINSLIE ©SailGP

Hattie with Sir Ben Ainslie on Great Britain SailGP Team F50

"The sport is changing rapidly, particularly with the foiling boats where innovation and development is constantly pushing boundaries. My ambition is to win the America's Cup and SailGP for Great Britain and keep loving being out there, as I have done from a very young age."

Hattie Rogers
May 2022

For our Centenary we had the motto: 'All things to all members'. In 100 years, I am confident we will be able to say the same about our Club. ⊗

25 HRH The Princess Royal Visits Centenary Regatta Day

On Saturday 18th June, Her Royal Highness The Princess Royal visited the Royal Lymington Yacht Club (RLymYC) for an impressive Regatta Day celebrating the Club's centenary.

The Centenary Regatta Day and 'Après Sail Festival' brought together members of all ages, their families and friends for a glorious celebration of one hundred years on the water. Flotillas of yachts, dinghies, motor boats and paddle craft took part in a wide variety of events during the day. Afterwards, members returned ashore for food, drinks, live music and fun activities including a Centenary Haybale Games on the green adjacent to the clubhouse.

RLymYC Commodore, Phil Lawrence, said: "We were honoured that our Patron, HRH The Princess Royal, was able to join over 800 members of all ages for our Centenary Regatta Day. We celebrated one hundred years of the Royal Lymington Yacht Club with a packed day of activities afloat and ashore.

"Out on the water Princess Anne reviewed our fleet of members' yachts and powerboats, many of which were dressed overall to celebrate the day. Keelboats raced for our prestigious PotterShip Trophy and the dinghy fleet raced in boisterous conditions. Our junior sailors were delighted to meet the Princess as she watched them learning the joys of boating.

"Back ashore, dozens of Club volunteers delivered a tremendous festival with food and drink, live music and fun activities on the green. It was fantastic

Patron of the Club since 1979, the Princess was welcomed by Her Majesty's Lord-Lieutenant of Hampshire, Mr. Nigel Atkinson, New Forest District Council's Vice-Chairman, Councillor Neville Penman, Mayor of Lymington, Councillor James Hoare, and the Club's Commodore, Phil Lawrence.

The Princess Royal was introduced to Club's Flag Officers, Centenary Regatta organisers and a number of young sailors, before heading out on the water in a RIB to tour the Regatta

Photo: Lymington Times and New Milton Advertiser/Steve West

All photographs in this chapter are courtesy of Sportography.tv unless stated otherwise.

A spectacular fleet of Members' yachts dressed overall in nautical flags, and motor cruisers anchored in lines on the Solent adjacent to the Club's Starting Platform for a Fleet Review by Her Royal Highness

to see so many members with a shared passion for boating - from the very youngest to those with over 50 years of membership enjoying the celebrations.

"We were delighted to showcase to Her Royal Highness the enormous range of varied activities and excellent facilities the Club has to offer. Whether your passion is motor cruisers, yachts, dinghies or paddle boards, junior sailing and training or a thriving social scene, the Royal Lymington Yacht Club has something for everyone."

The Princess Royal then took the opportunity to watch the prestigious PotterShip Race, an annual event where members compete for the glittering PotterShip Trophy (left), given by theClub's founder, Major Cyril Potter, in 1937. It is, of course, a Nef – a fully rigged medieval sailing merchantman and warship

The Princess Royal then had the opportunity to watch the Club's youngest sailors in more sheltered water closer to shore; a colourful display of pottering Lymington River Scows brightening up the grey sky.

HRH also spoke with the Boatmen...

...who were dressed as ice creams whilst delivering ice creams to the young sailors

Whilst out on the water, Her Royal Highness was introduced to the race and safety teams and watched the dinghy racing, where junior, youth and adult sailors were racing in windy conditions a lot stronger than originally forecast

After watching the start for the XODs the Princess Royal was treated to an impressive 'fly-past' by young Club member Hattie Rogers in her foiling Waszp. Hattie said, "The Centenary Regatta was a complete celebration of all types of racing and cruising. To sail in front of Her Royal Highness was an honour and very memorable."

On her return to the Club, Her Royal Highness named the Club's new RIB "Haven Jubilee"

The Princess Royal was presented with flowers and gifts from the Club by young member, Ruby Coster

Since becoming Patron of the Club in 1979, HRH The Princess Royal has made numerous working visits to the Club, including joining the crew in the ladies championship event, participating in RIB support of junior racing, and attending key events in the life of the Club, such as the commissioning of the new pontoon in 2016. The Princess Royal has been an enthusiastic visitor to the Club's special occasions and for a while kept her yacht on the river close to the Club.

The Royal Lymington Yacht Club is considered very much a home of yachting, dinghy sailing and motor boating, bringing together like-minded people with a love of the sea. The Club welcomes new members. To find out more, contact:
membership@rlymyc.org.uk or call **01590 672677**.

Appendix A : OLYMPIANS – MEMBERS SELECTED TO REPRESENT GREAT BRITAIN SINCE 1948

Year	Name	Class	Medal
2016	Nick Thompson	Laser	
2012	Ben Ainslie	Finn	Gold
2008	Ben Ainslie	Finn	Gold
2008	Nick Rogers	470	Silver
2008	Pippa Wilson	Yngling	Gold
2004	Ben Ainslie	Finn	Gold
2004	Nick Rogers	470	Silver
2000	Ben Ainslie	Laser	Gold
2000	Nick Rogers	470	
1996	Ben Ainslie	Laser	Silver
1992	Jez Fanstone	Reserve	
1992	Philip Lawrence	Star	
1988	Brin Vaile	Star	Gold
1984	Chris Law	Soling	
1984	Cathy Foster	470	
1980	Andrew Hurst	Not Known	
1980	Chris Law	Finn	
1976	Barry Dunning	Soling	
1976	Phil Crebbin	470	
1972	Stuart Jardine	Star	
1972	Barry Dunning	Soling	
1968	Stuart Jardine	Star	
1968	Adrian Jardine	5.5m	Bronze
1964	Stuart Jardine	Reserve	
1964	Adrian Jardine	5.5m	
1964	Graham Mann	Reserve	
1964	David Harris	Dragon	
1960	Stuart Jardine	Reserve	
1960	Adrian Jardine	Reserve	
1960	Graham Mann	Dragon	
1956	Richard Creagh-Osbourne	Finn	
1956	Graham Mann	Dragon	Bronze
1948	Sir Arthur MacDonald	Firefly	

Appendix B : COMMODORES AND VICE-COMMODORES

COMMODORES

1923–37 Maj. Cyril Potter
(Admiral 1939-41 and 1946–54)

1937–46
The Hon. Mrs C Brownlow

1946–54 Col. Hon. C.H.C.
(Henry) Guest (Admiral 1954–57)

1954–55

Maj. Bill Martineau

1955–58

Maj. H. W. Hall

1958–64

Cdr. Jack Bryans

1964–68

P.J.B. Perkins

1968–70

S.H.R. Clarke

1970–73

SurgV-A Sir Derek Steele-Perkins

1973–76

J.M.A. Paterson

1976–77

Howard French

1977–80

Chris Bowen

1980–83

Maj. Gen. Bill Woods

1983–86

Brig. D.R.L. Bright

1986–88

HH Judge Michael King

1988–92

AVM Sir Alan Boxer

1992–95

Maj. Peter Wilson

1995–98

Desmond Dewhurst

1998–2001

Gordon Simpson

2001–04

Capt. Andrew Tyrrell MN

2004–07

John Bence

2007–09
Geoff Holmes

2009–12
Rod Perry

2012–15
Phil Lawrence

2015–18
Dunlop Stewart

2018–21
Roger Garlick

2021–
Phil Lawrence

VICE-COMMODORES

1923–25 Maj. Gen. The Rt. Hon. J.B. Seely M.P.

1926–37 The Hon. Mrs C. Brownlow

1937–41 Col. The Hon. C.H.C. (Henry) Guest

1941–46 no name listed

1946–47 Capt. B.H. Goodhart

1947–54 Maj. Bill Martineau

1954–58 Cdr. Jack Bryans

1958–63 AVM G. Combe

1963–66 Cdr. M.H. Brown

1966–69 H. Goodhart

1969–71 D. E. Taylor

1971–75 W. E. Hampton

1975–78 AVM Sir Alan Boxer

1978–81 Derek Pitt-Pitts

1981–84 Noel Bond-Williams

1984–87 Eileen Caulcutt

1987–90 John Guillaume

1990–93 AVM Ted Hawkins

1993–95 Desmond Dewhurst

1995–99 Michael White

1999–2001 Capt. Andrew Tyrrell MN

2001–03 David Wansbrough

2003–07 Rod Perry

2007–10 Phil Batten

2010–13 John Mills

2013–15 Dunlop Stewart

2015–18 Clive Sparrow

2018–20 Robin Taunt

2020–22 John Tudor

2022– Stephen Crates

1984: WJS Launch

Dr Jonathan Rogers and Dr Tom McEwen started the scheme to give local children, for whom there were no other opportunities, a chance to get involved in sailing. Initially there were a couple of Scows, a Wayfarer, a 420 and some wooden Oppies. Wednesday was the chosen day as it was half day closing in the town and Jonathan's half day from the surgery. 1984: New Boats Jonathan built 4 scows from GRP shells and 3 of these were donated to be used by the junior sailing scheme. Also a couple of windfalls were acquired in the form of 2 GRP Oppies.

1985: Expansion

Local schools were informed and the response was overwhelming. Jonathan built the first four Avon Scows. Club Members offered to lend their Scows and soon there were 10 or 12 boats. Jonathan, a handful of Club Members and the Club Boatmen built a floating pontoon for the boats in front of the Club house.

1985: RYA

The RYA became interested in the scheme and sent John Stowell to give some advice on how to run the afternoons. He introduced the coloured dots system among many other things. Up to 75 children now were attending the afternoons. Jonathan took his Senior Instructor's exam so the Club could become a teaching establishment. Many Members became RYA qualified instructors.

1985: New Scows

The building of new Scows was taken on by John Claridge and many members loaned these Scows to the scheme. The problem of storing them was solved by Doug Baverstock building the first floating pontoon, the owners keeping them there in return for their use on Wednesdays. Stuart Jardine acquired an Army floating pontoon which was moored on the west side of the river and Jonathan's little Alice was anchored off with the doughnuts on board.

1986: New Pontoons

Doug Baverstock replaced the pontoons.

1987: More Scows

More Scows were bought by members for WJS to use and 4 fibre glass Oppies, built by Jeremy Rogers were donated by local businesses. Also 2 aluminium French Oppies.

1989: The White Cadet

The white Cadet was bought in 1989 and used most Wednesdays for several years.

1990: Oppies

12 new polypropylene Oppies were bought and the sails were donated by Wightlink .

1993/94: Scows

John Claridge built 14 hulls, Ruth Evans, Roger Wilson and Jonathan Rogers fitted them out during that winter. The first owners paid £2,000 for their boat including the sails with all the fitting-out down for no charge.

1994: WJS Cards
Roger and Jenny Wilson ran WJS between them for sixteen years. They were responsible for the Introduction of the WJS Card Scheme. Rowing was Introduced.

1994 Awarded the RYA Community Award.

1994: Lightweight Oppies
All the old fibreglass Oppies were replaced with polypropylene ones over a three year period with donations and sponsorship from Philip Grundy, The Acorn Trust, Mackenzie Associates, Jacques de la Cave, the Town Council and one or two other businesses. Martyn Hird co-ordinated all the sponsorship and also paid for a Scow.

1999: Growth
Up to 150 children now attending the afternoon. 2003: New Sponsor The Lymington Yacht Haven commenced their generous sponsorship of WJS which continues to this day. Powerboat training started this year.

2009: WJS 25th Anniversary Celebration
HRH The Princess Royal, our Patron, attended the afternoon. She was introduced to instructors, children RIB drivers and volunteers and was most interested to hear how the afternoons were organised.

2009: New RIB
RIB Golden Haven was acquired to support the running of WJS, sponsored by Lymington Yacht Haven.

2010: New Leader
Edward Harrison took over the running of WJS.

2010: Beyond The Barrier
Introduction of regular Scow racing beyond the wave barrier. Use of the RS Elite Freebie to take Children sailing out into the Solent.

2011: First Rowing Regatta
First rowing regatta held. The introduction of a new WJS Card Scheme, to align it more closely with the RYA National Sailing Scheme. Six RS Teras purchased with funds from Lymington Yacht Haven and three more boats subsidised by the Eric Twiname Trust. Two RS Visions also joined the fleet.

2012: Pink Fizz
RS Vision Pink Fizz bought with a legacy from Steve Etheridge.

2014: New Leader
Ali Husband took over running WJS. Optimist Hurst Castle was bought with a legacy from Bruce Kilpatrick.

2014: 30th Anniversary
Ten of the polypropylene Oppies were replaced. The 30th anniversary party was held in June. A large number of former volunteers attended the party. Many games were played and a large cake celebrated the occasion.

2019 35th Anniversary
HRH The Princess Royal joined us in June to celebrate the 35th Anniversary. She named a new Scow "Royal Coral" to mark the occasion.

2022 Youth Week
HRH The Princess Royal named a new Scow "Jonathan" in memory of co-founder of WJS Dr Jonathan Rogers in the presence of the Rogers family.

RS Aero's – a popular
and competitive class
of racing dinghy